CRUELTY

Frontispiece painting by Samuel M. Green

CRUELTY

By PHILIP P. HALLIE

 WESLEYAN UNIVERSITY PRESS
Middletown, Connecticut

Revised Edition

LIBRARY OF CONGRESS CATALOGING IN PUBLICATION DATA

Hallie, Philip Paul.
  Cruelty.

  Reprint. Originally published: The paradox of
cruelty. 1st ed. Middletown, Conn. : Wesleyan
University Press, 1969. With new introd. and postscript.
  Bibliography : p.
  Includes index.
  1. Cruelty.   I. Title.
BJ1535.C7H3   1982   179'.7   82–2040
ISBN 0–8195–6079–0 (pbk.)   AACR2

This book was first published in cloth under the title *The Paradox of Cruelty.*
Portions of the Introduction and Postscript to the paperback edition
first appeared in *The Hastings Center Report*, Vol. 11, No. 3, June 1981.

All inquiries and permissions requests should be addressed to the Publisher,
Wesleyan University Press, 110 Mt. Vernon Street, Middletown, Connecticut
06457

Distributed by Harper & Row Publishers, Keystone Industrial Park, Scranton,
Pennsylvania 18512

Library of Congress Catalog Card Number: 76–82535
Manufactured in the United States of America
First printing 1969; first Wesleyan Paperback edition 1982;
second printing, 1983

For Edwin C. Sanders,
who, even after all those cruelties,
is black and beautiful

The greatest defeat, in anything, is to forget, and above all to forget what it is that smashed you, and to let yourself be smashed without ever realizing how thoroughly devilish man can be. When our time is up, we people mustn't bear malice, but neither must we forget: we must tell the whole thing, without altering one word—

LOUIS-FERDINAND CÉLINE
Journey to the End of the Night

... we had little sayings that were passed on from generation to generation; some of them had probably come to us from as far back as the superstitious people hundreds of years before. When there was a flash of lightning that streaked across the sky a child would say, "The devil's beatin his wife." And when the deafening explosion of thunder followed, another child would reply, "Yeah, man, but she's fightin back." ...

RONALD L. FAIR
"We Who Came After"

CONTENTS

ILLUSTRATIONS

ACKNOWLEDGEMENTS

I am grateful to:

Alfred North Whitehead for the question he asked me one Fall day as we walked the streets of Cambridge, Massachusetts: "You say you love Physics and Poetry, young man, but have you achieved a *wedding* of the two?" That question posed by that man has informed my life and this book.

The Royal Society for the Prevention of Cruelty to Animals for their beautiful combination of legal cunning and moral compassion for the most defenseless victims of all.

The American Council of Learned Societies for a generous Research Fellowship during the Academic year 1966–67.

Mrs. Barbara Satton and Mrs. Tania Senff of the Wesleyan Center for Advanced Studies for their affectionate and stimulating presence during the making of this book.

Alex Knopp, who combines a Quaker's sense of moral presence with a splendid intellect, for his help with the key ideas of the book.

"Shep" Wheeler, whose capacity for hard work is as nothing compared to the gaiety of his wit, which helps us all to laugh, and thus to be free from life's cruelties.

Theodore R. Sarbin for a relationship too deep and personal to be put into words, but also for his immensely helpful guidance as a social psychologist and as a wise man.

My family, Louie Gabriel, Michelena Louise, and Doris Ann for helping me get to the heart of the matter by talking at our kitchen table. I am especially grateful to my daughter Michelena for always reminding me that all living things are members of the same family.

Finally, the man to whom this book is dedicated, a worthy descendant of Frederick Douglass. The mind and the heart of Edwin C. Sanders have made his forebear, Douglass, a flesh-and-blood presence in my life.

INTRODUCTION TO THE

PAPER EDITION

IF history is a nightmare, it is because there is so much cruelty in it. In peace as in war members of our species are cruel to one another, and human progress seems to consist not so much in diminishing that cruelty as in finding more impersonal and more efficient ways of crushing and grinding one another. Perhaps it is a long way from a cave man torturing his enemy or his woman to a Heinrich Himmler advising the leaders of the SS in a 1943 speech to be "decent" and "hard" in "exterminating a bacillus," the Jewish people. Still, across the changes those who need to understand the nightmare with better conceptual apparatus than the anecdotal sensationalism of a journalist feel the need to grasp the family resemblances between the various cruelties that make up so much of human history. Some of us need to see what it is that keeps recurring in the nightmare.

But if episodic journalism is a danger in the study of cruelty so is empty pattern-mongering. The dance of bloodless categories that broad theories present to us cannot show us the particular textures of the horrors. The sensationalistic journalists of cruelty know that we need to stay close to the episodes, close to the passions and actions of particular human beings if we are to penetrate the nightmare. And they are right. If I as a student of ethics were to spin out an intricate web of high-level abstractions regarding good and evil, and then fit into that web the particular evil we call "cruelty" I would be evading the truth that the horror-mongers never fail to see: that understanding cruelty is a cruel task. It is not a task for those who do not know by their own experience what a nightmare is.

And so, decades ago in my first efforts to keep the right cognitive distance from this immense and immediate subject, I decided to turn to etymological dictionaries. The origins of words are often rich in concrete and yet suggestive language. I found that the word "cruelty" comes from a variety of old words relating to the Latin *"crudus"* or "raw," and this word in turn is related to the Old Slavonic word for blood and the Sanskrit word for raw flesh. The origins of the word lie in the spilling of blood, in opening raw flesh.

But etymologies are not enough, just as history is not enough. The now is important too. And in present usage "cruelty" is not simply a reference to fleshy or bloody matters. It has much to do with awareness. A modern dictionary defines the word with the phrase "disposed to give pain to others." The patterns of past and present usage inform us that mental pain and physical bloodshed are the main ingredients of cruelty.

But how many times have we seen cruelty without bloodshed? How many times have we seen or heard about children and husbands and wives torturing each other not with hard weapons but with hard words? In Reska Weiss's *Journey Through Hell* there is a passage on one of the deepest cruelties the Nazis perpetrated upon extermination camp inmates. On a certain march "Urine and excreta poured down the prisoners' legs, and by nightfall the excrement, which had frozen to our limbs, gave off its stench. . . ." Weiss goes on to talk in terms not of local bodily pain or of bloodshed, but in other terms: ". . . We were really no longer human beings in the accepted sense. Not even animals, but putrefying corpses moving on two legs. . . ."[1]

Cruelty involves maiming a person's dignity, crushing a person's self-respect. Local bloodshed and pain are sometimes superficial matters as far as cruelty is concerned. Whips and bleeding flesh, like the dictionaries, do not take you very far into it. The understanding of cruelty lies in the depths of an understanding of the fragility of human dignity.

In excremental assault, in keeping prisoners from wiping themselves or from going to the latrine, or in making them drink from a toilet bowl full of excreta (and the excreta of the guards at that) bodily pain is nothing—disgust and humiliation are everything. Whether or not we are skeptics about ranking people or ranking pleasures or ranking pains, we human beings believe in hierarchies. There is a hierarchical gap between shit and me. And if you winced at the word in the last sentence, it is because you are "above" even using the word "shit." You are above walking around besmirched with feces on your face, on your hands, on your legs. Our dignity, whatever the origins and nature of that dignity may be, does not countenance it. We vulnerable creatures insist upon being "higher" than shit, and when we are not our lives are maimed at the very center, in the very depths, not merely wounded in some portion of our bodies.

And so it is necessary to turn away from dictionaries and look at the life of the word, its ways of being used in various contexts and circumstances. When you do this you not only discover that the victims of cruelty are often humiliated, not simply bloodied; you also discover that those victims are the ones who use the word the most often, not their victimizers. The word "cruelty" has an expressive function: it *expresses* pain and humiliation, does not simply describe these feelings. And these feelings are felt by the victims of cruelty, not by the perpetrators of it. Victimizers seldom use the word. There is a speech mentioned earlier that was delivered by Heinrich Himmler in Posen in 1943. Himmler was head of the Nazi SS and he was speaking to a select group of his immediate SS subordinates in a closed session. His subject was one of the most cruel episodes in the history of our species, but his language was free of such words as "cruel":

. . . Let me, in all frankness, mention a terribly hard chapter to you. Among ourselves, we can openly talk about it, though we will never speak a word of it in public. . . . I am speaking of the . . . extermination of the Jewish people. That is one of those things where the words come so easily. "The Jewish people will be exterminated," says every party member, "of course. It's in the program. . . . extermination. We'll take care of it." And then they come, these nice 80 million Germans, and every one of them has his

decent Jew. Sure, the others are swine, but this one is a fine Jew.
. . . Most of you will know what it means to have seen 100 corpses
together, or 500, or 1000. To have made one's way through that,
and—some instances of human weakness aside—to have remained
a decent person throughout, that is what has made us hard. That is
a page of glory in our history that never has been and never will
be written. . . .

And later he goes on: ". . . we can say that we fulfilled this heavi-
est of tasks in love to our people. And we suffered no harm in
our essence, in our soul, in our character. . . ."[2] There is no hint
of cruelty here, only "tasks in love" and "a page of glory in our
history." The victims of the Holocaust, the survivors of it, and
those who try to understand that page of glory from their point
of view speak of cruelty, but not the victimizers. The language
of the Nazis does not carry the pain and the humiliation that the
word "cruelty" carries. With a few changes, Himmler's speech
could have been about the extermination of rats in Germany.
Frederick Douglass in his autobiography *Life and Times* can
speak of cruelty when he speaks of the point of view of the black
slaves in the United States, but the slave holders and their over-
seers seldom use the word.

"Cruelty" is a perspectival word, and the perspective it expresses is usually the point of view of those who suffer, not of
those who inflict that suffering. The study of cruelty, whatever
else it may be, is a study of the victim's point of view on the
process of crushing human beings.

Having learned these things about the word, it became clear
to me that the study of cruelty required more than an understanding of the general meaning of that word. To find the right
cognitive distance from the subject, I found it necessary to dis-
tinguish various types of maiming and humiliation. Cruelty in
general is almost as vague as evil in general. And so, using what
I had learned about meanings, I found myself distinguishing
bloody, violent cruelty from bloodless, genteel harm-doing. A
chorus of venomous minds can sing its tuneless, hate-filled songs
to baffled black children almost to the point where blood breaks
through the victims' skins, but not quite. Chanted words outside
a school being desegregated need draw no blood from their vic-

tims; to be cruel they need only draw from the children's lips the question, "Why do they hate me so much?"

Another important distinction among cruelties is between cruel episodes and institutionalized maiming. A word, a stone can hurt for a moment, but the hurt can fade in time; a persistent, traditional way of degrading human beings, by slavery or by Jim Crow behavior or by genocidal hatred, does not fade in time. It endures beyond the fading moment, so that even its victims sometimes become their own victimizers, sucking their feelings of inferiority or even disgust with themselves with their mothers' milk.

Still, having noticed these distinctions and generalizations, I found myself nagged by the feeling that I had not understood the dynamism of the nightmare. I was classifying, sorting out symptoms; but symptoms are signals, and what were these symptoms signals of? I felt like a person who had been studying cancer by sorting out brief pains from persistent pains, pains in the belly from pains in the head. I was being superficial, because I was not seeing what triggers these various kinds of maimings.

And then one day I was reading *Life and Times*, one of the great autobiographies of western civilization. I came across a passage on the origins of black enslavement, or at least the origins of Douglass's enslavement. He was asking himself: "How can my master keep me enslaved?" Then the answer came to him: ". . . The right to take my earnings was the right of the robber. He had the power to compel me to give him the fruits of my labor, and this *power* was his only right in the case. . . ."[3] As a slave he was systematically humiliated and used. Where did these indignities come from? On the first day of the year 1836 Douglass found himself thinking: ". . . My faculties and powers of body and soul are not my own, but are the property of a fellow-mortal in no sense superior to me, except that he has the physical power to compel me to be owned and controlled by him. By the combined physical force of the community I am his slave —a slave for life. . . ."[4]

There is a difference between the strong and the weak, and

in the process of cruelty that difference is transformed into humiliation and suffering for the weak. Whatever intimacies there
may be in the cruel relationship (and love and hatred can be
cruel) there is the pathos of distance in it, the feeling of fatal
difference. The essay that follows is an attempt to see how power
becomes pathos.

—January 1982

CRUELTY

INTRODUCTION

Early in his book *Kon-Tiki* Thor Heyerdahl tells how coldly he was received when he tried to get even a reading for a treatise on a vast topic. The argument of the treatise was that certain South Americans crossed four thousand miles of Pacific waters to land in the South Sea Islands sometime between 500 A.D. and 1100 A.D. Anthropologists told him that such a topic was too large to be handled professionally—after all, it involved two different cultures, Polynesia and Peru; they told him to specialize in either Polynesia *or* South America and "not mix up two separate anthropological areas."[1] When he came to a friend for advice and comfort, he was told that specialists

> ... don't believe in a method of work which cuts into every field of science from botany to archaeology. They limit their own scope in order to be able to dig in the depths with more concentration for details. Modern research demands that every special branch shall dig in its own hole. It's not usual for anyone to sort out what comes up out of the holes and try to put it all together."[2]

And his friend showed him a heavy manuscript that had been immediately accepted for publication—it was on bird design in Chinese peasant embroidery.

But Heyerdahl could not deal with his topic within one discipline; it was too complex; it had to be approached in various ways. To have tried to prove his point within a single discipline would have been "like doing a puzzle and only using the pieces of one color."[3] In the end he had to go *around* the various disci-

3

plines by constructing a raft of fresh balsa wood and sailing on it from Peru to the Polynesian islands in exactly the same way his treatise had claimed the South Americans had done it. On a raft with a simple sail he put himself and a small crew, and, moved only by prevailing winds and currents, he went from Peru to the South Sea Islands, with only enough steering to keep the raft afloat.

For a long time I have had a conviction too complex to explore in a scientific treatise. I have believed that pain is only a small part of cruelty, only a symptom of a condition that is more important to understand than the pain itself. I have believed that just as in diagnostic medicine pain is a part of a syndrome, so in cases of cruelty pain is part of a complex relationship between the victimizer and the victim. However, definitions of "cruelty" have to do only with the infliction of pain. *The Concise Oxford Dictionary* defines the adjective "cruel" as "indifferent to, delighting in, another's pain";[4] and the unabridged *Oxford English Dictionary* defines cruelty as a "disposition to inflict suffering."[5] Experience and reading had convinced me that a fuller understanding of this topic would not only reveal other aspects than suffering, but might show us how to mitigate cruelty, just as doctors learn to treat a disease through understanding it more fully.

And yet this topic was even more vast and complex than Heyerdahl's, and unlike Heyerdahl I was a specialist myself. This meant I had to emerge from the traditional confines of my own specialty, and approach a body of ideas as vast as the Pacific. I could not, therefore, steam or fly across this ocean on a carefully predetermined course—this would have been as irrelevant to a full understanding of the topic of cruelty as it would have been had Heyerdahl done it to prove *his* point.

And so I took my convictions on cruelty and pain, and of them made a philosopher's raft—for I was trained as a philosopher. But these were not the only components of my raft. I had a Sceptic's distrust of high-flown definitions or theories that are not useful for solving urgent problems, that make neat patterns but do not do any work. To be more precise, I was a Montaignian sceptic, who believed that "it is always man we are dealing with,"[6] not pure theories alone, which can be interpreted by men in as many ways as Plato's philosophy and Christianity have been interpreted. I believed that the best way to understand theories is to see how men illustrate them in their actions.

Upon these convictions, as upon a raft, I put myself, and I set out toward my goal: a fuller understanding of cruelty than I had hitherto encountered. My prevailing winds and currents were my abiding interest in art, literature, psychology, and history, and I was hoping that, if I maintained only enough steerageway to keep my raft afloat, they might bring me to that understanding. I knew that one must seek only that degree of precision appropriate to one's topic. Understanding cruelty involves understanding the relationships between life and death, and these are relationships that are oversimplified uselessly by precise theories. The word "cruelty" is a chameleon-word, dependent for its specific meaning upon its contexts—it is as much a chameleon-word as the words "life" and "death." And so I would not try to study all kinds of cruelty, but only two: human cruelties visited upon human beings (though I had learned much from the actions and publications of societies dedicated to the prevention of cruelty to animals); and fatal cruelties, such cruelties as are suggested by the opening sentence of Poe's "The Pit and the Pendulum": "I was sick—sick unto death with that long agony."

I was not going to spend much time probing the depths of the waters I was crossing—though living creatures from those depths would, I was sure, leap onto my raft, as they had leapt onto Heyerdahl's. The depths I would for the most part leave to the specialists with the right training and equipment. Nor was I going to navigate by the stars of ethical ideals. My Montaignian Scepticism about men who build castles in the air and live in slime here below made me suspicious of these. After all, much cruelty has been perpetrated in the name of such ideals, and though they are often powerful forces on men's lives, their influence on a given action is sometimes hard to predict. What men do involves so many other factors that we had better study their actions, not one ambiguous aspect of their actions.

My only star would be cruelty itself—mortal maiming. Cruelty would be to me like the North Star sailors use to help determine their position; its position relative to their horizons tells them where they are in the world. If you do not see the victims of cruelty and can explain cruelty away and live with destruction comfortably, you are adrift as far as your understanding of history is concerned.

Of course, if you become obsessed with cruelty, you may become too fascinated by it to find your way in the world. Life is so full of the willful maiming of lives, so full of victims, that you may begin to think that you are in Hell, not navigating on a planet that does have some benign moments. Meat may become distasteful to you, since many animals are bled slowly; nature may become a scene of unceasing torture—she often maims her children slowly, and kills them all; and man's life in human society may become heartbreaking—losers in competition of all sorts are maimed in varying degrees. To be obsessed with cruelty is to hate the law for its delays and its slow punishments, even (or *especially*) when the punishments are "just." And to be obsessed with cruelty is to hate crime and its horrors because of those who suffer from them.

No, my Pole Star would not be an obsession. The person who sees only the faces of victims in nature and society becomes cruel himself—the full-time torturer and destroyer of himself.

Just as Heyerdahl believed that somehow he would get to the Polynesian islands with permissive guidance and with happy-go-lucky equipment, so I believed that I would terminate and climax my exploratory study of cruelty with an examination of the cruelties perpetrated upon the black people of my country, America. I knew that in the beginning I would use artistic and literary fictions to approach the understanding I sought, but I also knew that in the end I would elucidate and test these fictions in the history of flesh and blood. I believed that one of the most penetrating cruelties ever perpetrated by my country was done upon our black people, and I knew that the agony America was undergoing at the time of my study would have to confirm my explanation of cruelty or I would reject it immediately.

A philosopher dealing with emotion-charged problems like this finds it necessary to use approaches that are not appropriate to the traditional, perennial problems of Philosophy (problems like whether there is an external world or whether there are other minds). Such problems give us a great deal of time for finding their solutions because they are not practically or emotively *pressing*. But understanding man's desire to kill his fellow-man and trying to thwart that desire are urgent problems; they require special methods.

And so the approach used in this book is not easy to describe in the traditional terms of the history of philosophy. We can call it that of "the interpreted image." It uses pictures centrally, and makes an analysis of these pictures that never loses sight of the fact that an image can make a great number of emotion-charged facts clear. It is no accident that this is one of the few philosophy books ever written in which illustrations play a central role. Whatever analysis there is in this book is very closely involved with the pictures that appear here, especially the pictures of Hogarth's engravings and the photograph of Frederick Douglass.

Men have for centuries been suspicious of images, not only for religious reasons, but for scientific ones. Images can obstruct careful investigation; for instance, Earth, Air, Fire, and Water had to be rejected as the ultimate elements of reality because they were obstacles to detailed analysis and straightforward observation. But the images we shall be using are meant to be guides to an understanding of a large number of facts that might otherwise not be understood.

In psychology, "role theory" uses images relating to the theater to guide our search for facts about human behavior in society. When these images and their interpretation lose their ability to guide us and to help us comprehend the relationships between facts, they will have to be replaced by more useful images and interpretations. A more complex set of images than those used in role theory is used in this book: its main images are of chains, castles, and machines; and it uses subsidiary images, like that of the North Star and the Devil.

These are emblems that are not drawn from any one institution or activity, but they help bring together facts that were previously disparate, and they help us to see cruelty more fully and more lucidly than any other set of emblems I know. When they begin to obstruct our study of the facts regarding man's inhumanity to man they should be replaced. Above all, we must not stop trying to examine matters of life and death simply because they are difficult to settle.

In studying such matters, precision and rigorous proof can narrow our understanding so severely as to blind us to their full content. And so instead of trying to define our terms with a precision that ignores the range of such chameleon-words as "cruelty," and instead of trying to move sure-footedly from evidently true premises to evidently true conclusions, we shall try to understand cruelty by the progressive clarification of images. The first chapter will introduce those images, not as precise truths, but as possibly useful guidelines for what comes afterwards. Each successive chapter will be not a step in a proof but a step toward a clarification of the images. And the concluding chapter will not state supposedly proven, rigorous certainties; it will rather exhibit or show forth the key images of the book in their factual richness. It may show the critical reader how inadequate the images are compared to other ways of comprehending vast human issues, but many things worth doing involve danger. Surely risks are worth taking when what we are after is a useful vision of a momentous aspect of human history.

PHILIP P. HALLIE

Passover, 1969

HOGARTH ON THE POWER

OF THE WEAK

CONSIDER the first plate of William Hogarth's most carefully wrought "progress" or sequence of scenes, his *Marriage à la Mode*. The scene is the signing of a marriage contract, and the two foci of that picture are the fathers at the table and the children on the divan. A pompous nobleman (see the coronet on his crutches, and on so many other things in his room) Lord Squanderfield, as wasteful as he is muddle-headed, with the mish-mash of architectural styles in that building of his to be seen through his window, this man is selling his son's title and person to a canny alderman for cash; and the alderman is not losing a daughter, but gaining a titled son-in-law. The fathers have sentimental, social, and financial power over their offspring, and are using it on those two youthful figures with their backs turned to each other.

In the foreground, at the young nobleman's feet, two dogs are chained to each other with an absurdly heavy chain, and one of the dogs has a coronet on his body, to drive home the parallelism between the condition of the young people and the condition of the dogs, and also to emphasize the motif (and the pomposity) of the coronet. Two people are being forced to marry, are being bound to each other in a quietly cruel situation. The victims are on one side of the picture, the victimizers on the other, with the young lawyer Silvertongue, who is beginning his seduction of the

9

Marriage à la Mode, Plate I

girl, making the transition. One of the victims, the girl, is playing distractedly with her (wedding?) ring, and listening to Silvertongue the seducer; the other victim has turned his back to his spouse, and is perhaps looking in the mirror like the dandy he is (in the engravings his mirror-image looks mock-modestly downward under his gaze).

The quiet cruelty in the foreground contrasts with the bloody, physical cruelty in the background, in those paintings above the young people. Surrounding the oval picture of Medusa (whose power is so great as to petrify her victims) is a picture of Saint Lawrence roasting on a Roman gridiron, Saint Agnes martyred after she rejected *her* noble suitor, and Cain killing Abel (as Councillor Silvertongue will kill the young Dangerfield). On the other wall, behind Silvertongue, there is the martyrdom of Saint Sebastian (the quill in Silvertongue's hand, pointed at his own heart, resembles the arrows in Sebastian), and there are other scenes of physical destruction.

Behind the table where the money is being exchanged is a portrait of a noble, military hero, a member of the Squanderfield line, if the coronet on the frame means anything. On this side of the room are the victimizers, the powerful ones, curiously separate from their victims, though we know that their power is having its effects on them. In physics power involves the speedy overcoming of resistance, and all the people on this side of the painting have readily overcome any resistance the young people might have offered.

At this point I must quote the great eighteenth-century commentator on Hogarth's engravings, G. C. Lichtenberg. His description of that nobleman in the background is typical of his humor and sensitivity, and summarizes the physical violence and grandeur that pervade the picture of

> . . . the man whose portrait on the wall there occupies the space of four murder stories . . . is a family hero, and whoever cares to see wind, storm, and thunder without hearing them, should pause before this picture. The hero in a sort of wig which . . . would . . . rightly be regarded as belonging among the thunder clouds, is in the midst of the turmoil of battle . . . he stands at the head of his army . . . .With a mien full of self-approval, he surveys the rich harvest of victory [he is looking toward the young people]. . . .

Marriage à la Mode, Plate I (detail)

He stands there inspiring awe, and could even defy that comet's tail which is hovering above him. . . . Below, a cannon goes off right under the hero's cloak, almost as if the explosion emanated from his trouser pocket.[1]

In the chapter on the Gothic Tale we shall see how wild weather creates and symbolizes awe-ful sensations (that vast, indefinite power of "wind, storm, and thunder without hearing them . . . "). Here it is enough to say that this first picture of Hogarth's most mature progress is an example of peaceful, polite cruelty and bloody victimization. The background is bloody and almost noisy with screams, cannons, storms, etc.; the foreground is decorous, *comme il faut*, and Councillor Silvertongue with his quill makes the transition between the foreground and the background as firmly as he makes the transition between the victims and their victimizers. For our purposes, this first picture exemplifies the basic ideas of this book.

It shows that cruelty can be quiet as well as dramatic, decorous as well as brutal, that it involves the power of the strong being exerted against the often mild resistance of the weak, and that it is possible for the victimizers to seem isolated from their victims, as the two fathers are from their children, and as the "family hero" is from his vanquished enemy.

But it also shows that people can victimize each other *without explicitly intending to do so*. They can victimize each other for other reasons than sadistic pleasure. They can do so for money, for social position, for comfort, etc. But they are still maiming the victim slowly, even though they are not thinking about maiming him—even though they are thinking about the money or the position or the comfort.

There is a curious innocence to some kinds of victimization, a disregard of the effects on the victim, a concentration on one's own motives, that announces the separation, the abyss that can exist between the victim and his victimizer. He does not need to want to hurt his victim—he needs only to want something that requires him to hurt the victim. He can get what he wants in total disregard of the ruin he is inflicting.

And so, a man can be cruel without having cruelty as his main or even his subsidiary aim. He can be cruel by omission and by commission—all at once. He can disregard the victim in a sincere desire to do something good (at least for himself), something whose goodness is more important to him than is the maiming he is bringing about. That something good can be so important to him that he sees nothing but the good or the beneficial. He can say: After all, who knows what the future will bring? These young people might grow to love each other—in time, with all those social amenities that will come from their marriage. And even the victims, the young people, might find themselves thinking along the lines of their fathers—even while they turn their backs upon each other in disregard or disdain.

All of this simply means that any understanding of cruelty should leave out the phrase "intention to hurt"—the intention may not be there, but the maiming may be as substantial as if it were there. In this book, which emphasizes the victim, the main thing is that maiming is done, not the accident of whether the person who does the maiming is doing it for the sake of maiming itself. Cruelty is for us the infliction of ruin, whatever the "motives." A person may be just as much ruined by a well-meaning father as he is by a sadist. The missionaries who destroyed the lives of natives in order to save their souls, even when the natives disagreed (or because the natives disagreed) with their eschatology—these missionaries were just as cruel to the natives as a sadist would have been, though they were quite innocent, let us say, of wanting to hurt people for the sake of hurting them. Intentions are not as important as ruination.

But how can we want the best and do the worst *in the act* of finding the best? We must face the paradox involved in this question.

But you don't "face" a paradox in any but a highly abstruse way. You face particular events, and you find, perhaps, paradoxes in them. Ordinary "clarity" involves light, and therefore vision, often in the plain, physical sense of these words; and light falls on particular objects and illumines them—at least if they *are* clear to us. In order to see this deep and complex matter of cruelty more clearly, we have begun to look at some pictures.

William Hogarth was born and died in the England of the eighteenth century during the English Enlightenment. He and many of his contemporaries cherished lucid, palpable fact more than they did the dark Juggernaut of tradition or the purple passages of "enthusiasm" religions, like Methodism. He was part of an age that loved what his friend Henry Fielding called "Examples" and despised the commands that get their power from old habits and self-indulgent, orgiastic religious passions. In the first sentence of the first book of *Joseph Andrews* Fielding wrote:

> It is a trite but true Observation, that Examples work more forcibly on the Mind than Precepts.[2]

And in Hogarth's notes towards an autobiography we find a similar idea:

> Occular [*sic*] demonstration will convince . . . sooner than ten thousand Vols . . . [3]

Of course what both of them were talking about was not simple clarity, physical light falling on particular things, but also the power to influence human actions. The English Enlightenment wanted the kind of clarity that influences men's behavior (not the kind of clarity that a mathematician like Descartes would enjoy in the solitary contemplation of the pure sciences).

Hogarth knew the sick orphans and the gin-soaked people of London, and Fielding was justice of the peace for the counties of Middlesex and Westminster. Like so many other Englishmen, they saw the horrible waste of life that was commonplace around them, and they saw it not in terms of an evil that iron tradition and the innate sinfulness of the passions made fixed and unchangeable; they saw everything around them as *malleable*. They believed that once the facts are clearly seen in their powerful particularity, their here-and-nowness, they can be changed if they are destroying life; and once we know they can be changed, they *will* be changed. Daniel Defoe, who also saw his country in all of its particular horrors, wrote on December 26, 1706, "England, bad as she is, is yet a reforming Nation." And M. Dorothy George in her *London Life in the Eighteenth Century* quite rightly puts this remark at the head of her Introduction to that century.[4] Reform, change, all in the service of changing human behavior to avoid the waste of life, this was Hogarth's version of "Enlightenment." In London's gutters babies were being abandoned in large numbers; in the drunken and filthy poor districts, in the deadly hospitals life was being destroyed, not by accident and not by necessity, but because people were not acting usefully as far as preserving the fullness of life was concerned. This is what they all meant by the phrase "waste of life." And Defoe, Fielding, and Hogarth, amongst many others, turned their art to the making of "Examples" or what Hogarth called "Occular demonstrations," so that lives could be saved in this malleable world.

True, we are talking about artists, and as artists they were interested in making artifacts that were pleasing in themselves, well made. They were not philistines, semi-skillful hands in the service of a dreary didacticism; they wanted to please as well as instruct. Hogarth's *Analysis of Beauty* is one of the most important eighteenth-century essays on art. Partly because they pleased, they still live—didacticism is not in itself very dear to man, though it can have its moments. Another friend of Hogarth, the actor David Garrick, put the moral and esthetic force of Hogarth rather neatly on Hogarth's tombstone in Cheswick:

> Farewell, great painter of mankind
> Who reach'd the noblest point of art;
> Whose pictur'd morals charm the mind
> And through the eye correct the heart.

Delight and instruction—they were, thank God, men, not machines.

But their principles are important to the principles of this book, and so I have delayed its argument to mention them. They believed in the power of particular cases when they are effectively used, and they were impatient with abstractions that started from precepts, commands that came from the dark tar-pits of human habits, traditions, and passions. They wanted to see and show the world, and they were sure that once this happened men would make progress toward changing it. And what they meant by progress was the elimination of the waste of life.

All of these old-fashioned ideas are the basic ideas of this book. Where this book differs from William Hogarth, incidentally, is in the degree of confidence it reposes in the power of examples to change human behavior. Hogarth had great faith that "occular demonstration" would change people. This book holds little hope for the motivating power of examples, except when their force is exerted upon a "well-disposed" or already converted mind. This book uses examples to help show that the main hope for progress in the diminution of the waste of life lies in the power of the would-be *victim*. If he has no power, I have little hope for him. If he has power (and his power *might* be activated or enhanced by examples he has seen), then there is hope. Examples will help clear up the nature of cruelty or victimization; they will not by themselves clear the world of cruelty or victimization. It is up to victims and their allies to do this.

Most treatises on ethics (of which this is not one) do not find their principles in their examples; they find their examples in their principles—they are single-mindedly abstract. The main kinds of ethical theories depend upon "criteria" for distinguishing right from wrong, criteria that presumably only the strong need grasp. Deontological (duty-ethics), eudemonistic (consequences in terms of pleasure and pain) and sentimental (benevolence) theories put all the power for ethical decision in the hands of the stronger, the philosopher-king. And he gets all his power from these criteria or principles. This book finds the capacity to tell right from wrong not in Kant's Duty or Categorical Imperative, nor in Bentham's pleasure-pain calculations, nor in Hutcheson's and Hume's moral sense or benevolence. It finds that power mainly in the sensibilities of the victims or would-be victims. It sees ethics not only as a matter of criteria used by the powerful, but mainly as a matter of pressures of all sorts used by the powerless against their tormentors. Ethics is the way the weak limit the strong, not simply the way the strong philosophize amongst themselves. But we shall not be attacking all those modes of celestial navigation.

We have already discussed the first picture of *Marriage à la Mode*, a product of Hogarth's rich middle period of productivity, and in doing so we have picked out some of the main features of cruelty, at least as we shall be studying it. Cruelty is the smashing of the weak by the strong, either peacefully, civilly, or noisily, bloodily. Those two dogs in the foreground, chained to each other, are enduring a kind of cruelty somewhere in between the quiet and the loud, but they "suffer" in their way, just as the other weak ones in that picture suffer in their several ways.

The fatal consequences of these cruelties are visible in the facing plate, the last one of the *Marriage à la Mode* series. We must go on to another. In 1751 Hogarth was doing engravings less rich, less complex and less pleasing than the famous progresses he had been doing until 1747. In 1751 he did *Beer Street* and *Gin Lane*. The cheapness and the ready availability of gin were destroying lives in large numbers—especially amongst the desperate poor, who for a few pennies and with no effort could exorcise their desperation and destroy their lives and the lives of their children in the process. In 1750, in St. Giles, London, every fourth house was a gin shop for the poor, and a certain Judith Dufour took her two-year old child out of the workhouse, where she had just been washed and clothed, strangled her, left her in a ditch, and sold her clothes for gin money. Those various interests who were keeping gin cheap and available were destroying the lives of the weakest members of society, the poor, as surely as the two fathers were destroying their fashionable children, as surely as Medusa destroyed her victims.

In notes now in the British Museum Hogarth explained these two plates. Here he wanted, as far as cheap gin was concerned,

> . . . every circumstance of its horrid effects brought to view in terorem [*sic*] nothing but Poverty Idleness misery and pain. . . . Distress even to madness and death and not a house in tolerable condition but Pawnbrokers and the Gin Shop.[5]

At this time in his life, after the period in which he had done *A Harlot's Progress*, *A Rake's Progress*, and his masterpiece, *Mar-*

Marriage à la Mode, Plate VI

riage à la Mode, indignation, anger, and help for the victim were far more important to Hogarth than "great correctness of drawing or fine Engraving." On the contrary, he went on, these would make the engravings too expensive, "out of the reach of those for whom they were chiefly intended."[6] In this last period of his life, his didacticism in defense of the weak was often naked of careful design and esthetic intent. He wanted mainly to change a cruel situation, and he worked to change it not only in his engravings but in his own actions against the vested interests defending cheap gin.

In this same year of 1751 he produced *The Four Stages of Cruelty*. About these four engravings he said, near his remarks on the gin engravings,

> The four stages of cruelty were done in hopes of preventing in some degree cruel treatment of poor Animals which make the streets of London more disagreeable to the human mind, than anything whatever, the very describing of which gives pain but this could not be done in to[o] strong a manner as the most stony heart were meant to be affected by them.[7]

Between 1732 and 1746 he had done his inexhaustible and gracious progresses; now in his last period (between 1747 and 1764, when he died) he was willing to cause pain in his readers so that "the most stony heart" could be moved to prevent the maiming of the ultimate victims, the weakest voyagers in human society, the animals in the streets. He was willing to use the *in terrorem* (as he put it) technique to defend these creatures just as he had been using it to defend the poor.

But in the cruelty engravings, the victimizer was clearer than he was in *Gin Lane*, or in the first plate of *Marriage*. Indeed, those who were making gin so readily available were absent from the scene, and the poor were victimizing themselves, at least to all appearances. But in the cruelty engravings, we have a single, clearly identifiable villain, Tom Nero, and we witness his progress from cruelty to cruelty in a situation wherein the victimizer is always in the foreground.

Glance over the whole series. Notice that the first three plates take place in the streets, first under a light sky, then under a darker sky with a large cloud in it, then under a night sky

The Four Stages of Cruelty
First Stage of Cruelty

inhabited by a bat and an owl, a sky worthy of a horror tale. The fourth engraving is indoors, in a round room. As is usual with Hogarth his backgrounds tell as much as his foregrounds. The skies show Nero's condition, and so does that room. At first he is free to act: the streets are open to him. But finally he is totally incapable of acting upon anybody. The world is closing in on him. The world is doing to him what he has been doing to his victims: capturing them and slowly destroying them.

What was in the background of our *Marriage* pictures, noisy or violent cruelty, is in the foreground of these pictures. And what is happening is not the constraint of minds or personal predilections for the sake of the victimizer's absent-minded ego- tism. What is happening is the maiming of bodies for the sheer satisfaction of doing just that—at least this is what is happening in the first two plates. The absent-minded innocence that those two fathers exhibit while they are manacling their children to each other is nowhere to be seen here. As we have noticed, maim- ing for the joy of maiming, destroying for the joy of destroying, and for no ulterior motive, is as cruel as "practical" cruelty. Let us consider this sadistic kind of cruelty.

All the animals being victimized in that first plate are cap- tured and isolated from help or escape. In order to victimize a creature you have to have it "in your power"—you have to sequester it. If that creature could get away or get help it would no longer be passive enough to be a victim—it would be an active enemy or an active, running prey. The main elements of cruelty are action and passion, doing and undergoing, and an active victim does not have the passivity that slow maiming demands. Look at the central figures of the plate under the lamp. That dog whose right hind leg Tom Nero holds, and into whose anus Nero has rammed the arrowhead, is a powerful dog, with a fairly large chest and a thick neck. If Tom were not holding that leg, and if his helpers were not holding that rope taut and that other leg, we would not be witnessing cruelty—we would be wit- nessing a battle. The dog is resisting in much the same ineffectual way as those two young people in the *Marriage*, and it is likely that his resistance is intensifying his suffering and hastening his destruction, just as their ineffectual resistance is aggravating the

First Stage of Cruelty (detail)

cruelty being done them. The street is fairly crowded with people, but he is nonetheless isolated, imprisoned, in the power of those three boys. All the other creatures in the plate are also imprisoned, though there are no visible walls; all of them have lost their freedom of bodily action as surely as those two chained dogs in the first plate of *Marriage*.

As in rococo works (and Hogarth is in some ways a rococo artist), Hogarth has captured a fleeting moment, a part of a whole action, the moment when that action was at its height. But because there is no sense of repose in such art, we feel that this is only a moment in a process, a part of a longer action.

Cruelty not only involves captivity; it also takes time, just as one "does time" in a prison. This is central to one's suffering; a victim of cruelty "does time," endures a process. And a process that ends in horror often begins gently. In fact, the gentleness helps put the victim in the power of his oppressor. The boy in the lower right hand corner is tying a bone to the tail of the dog licking his hand, and the boy is smiling too, although it is a dark smile. All this gentleness is the gateway to the torture chamber, and is as much a part of cruelty, is just as cruel, just as destructive of its victim as that moment of action before the large post. Momentary kindness often is a part of the cruel act; cruelty can be going on when there is not yet any dramatic pain.

In short, *the absence of dramatic pain does not mean the absence of cruelty*. True, when there is pain being inflicted by another there usually is cruelty—the feeling of pain can be a reliable symptom of cruelty. But the absence of that feeling indicates nothing about whether cruelty is happening. To know *this* we must know what tying a bone to a dog's tail *means*; we must know that what follows it usually is the tearing out of that tail by the roots, especially if there are very hungry dogs nearby, dogs that cannot be driven off since they are attacking from behind. To know that we are witnessing an act of cruelty is to know how the actions as well as the passions of the victim will be affected by what is happening now.

In short, cruelty is not simply the infliction of pain. It is a set of actions and passions that issue in certain actions and passions, and only one of these passions is pain. Gentleness can be

The Four Stages of Cruelty
Second Stage of Cruelty

another. The process of cruelty is a process in which pain may often be an element, and sometimes, as we have been noticing, is not an element at all.

What is always an important part of the cruel action is rendering the resistance of the victim ineffectual, making him passive. What is crucial to cruelty is the process of maiming the ordinary patterns of behavior that are the victim's ways of living. Sometimes it takes long observation to see that maiming; for instance, one must look through the whole progress of *Marriage* in order to see the destruction of these two young people. But sometimes one can see this faster, at a glance; for instance, one sees this at once when one looks at that dog with the arrow up his anus, or when one looks at that bird immediately above him with the burnt stick in his eye, or when one looks at those two cats suspended against each other over the second pole, or when one looks above them at that cat floating in the sky on fragile balloons with his vacant face looking at us.

The point of all this is that cruelty is the maiming of ways of living; it does not simply consist of momentary, disconnected inflicted pains. A cat does not easily fly on balloon-wings, nor does it happily allow itself to be suspended in mid-air against another equally terrified cat. Cats need footing. Dogs, like the one in Nero's power, do not function normally suspended in air, pulled by a rope, with an arrow up their anus. All of this is obvious, but the point is crucial: cruelty is a question of the whole experience and behavior of its victim, not just a question of its momentary pains. Cruelty is the maiming of a whole life, at least when the cruelty is heavy, and that maiming takes place in captivity, or else the oppressor would not have enough power over the victim to make so radical an alteration upon him.

From the oppressor's point of view, even in this sort of sadistic or pure cruelty, it is not only the moment of pain that is pleasing; it is the power over a creature's whole life. The victim-izer experiences the whole process and enjoys that whole process, including the entrance into the torture chamber, *and* the pain expressed in his victim's facial and bodily contortions. He enjoys the slow maiming of a life, and enjoys his own power over that life. The smile of that boy tying the bone to the dog's tail is a smile of pleasure that resembles the villain's pleasure in a melo-drama when he says, "You are in my power, my proud beauty!" and laughs. That laugh in its various forms in literature and life expresses his exhilaration with his power to change a whole life radically. The oppressor who acts with quiet cruelty, like the fathers in the *Marriage*, does not experience exhilaration—he is merely indifferent to the maiming, as the fathers are indifferent to the maiming they are perpetrating on their children; their attention is on other matters.

We have seen then that cruelty in that first plate is a process of which pain is an element, but of which the sequestered maim-ing of a way of life is of great importance. For the victim at least cruelty is a matter of life and death, not simply a matter of momentary pain. For his victimizer the process may not be so important—after all, no one is seizing him and smashing his way of life. On the contrary, he seems to be free of hindrance, an active being realizing his whims vigorously on the bodies and minds of his victims.

But to stop here is to ignore not only the rest of the series and Hogarth's stated intentions in drawing it, but to ignore a very important part of that first engraving. To Nero's left a boy is drawing the consequences of Nero's actions in the form of Nero hanging by the neck on the gallows. In front of Nero is a young man holding Nero's wrist in one hand and a tart for a bribe in the other. The prison walls are not high enough; the power of Nero over the life of that animal is not unlimited. The victim has allies, and they are expressing allegiance in two ways: one im-mediate and the other long-term. The hanging is a matter of public, distant consequences; the tart and that hand on Nero's wrist are matters of personal, immediate resistance.

All in all that group of boys around that dog expresses both the weakness of the victim and his strength. In that group Ho-garth is beginning to redress the imbalance of power between the victim and its victimizer. And in doing this he introduces another element into the process of cruelty—the outsider. He shows us that cruelty has three participants, not simply a strong one and a weak one. There are other powers at work in the world than those at work in that would-be prison. And it is the effect of the outsider, of his compassion and of his power to set public forces into motion, that Hogarth uses to soften "the most stony heart" in the form of a threat *in terrorem*.

But the center of that central group is the dog, the victim. The power of the outsider and the power of the victimizer revolve around him.

Jacques Callot, in some ways Hogarth's master as an engraver, had done a similar scene in a 1635 engraving called *The Temptation of St. Anthony*. In Callot's engraving a devil is riding (facing backwards) a goat-legged, winged creature, and with his left hand he is holding its tail. He is shoving an arrow up his rectum with his right hand. In the impressions I have seen of this engraving, one cannot make out the face of the devil's victim, let alone see any sign of the victim's suffering. But in Hogarth's engraving the face of that tortured dog is the most contorted and eloquent face in the plate, and the strong diagonal lines that move down from the arrow and down from the right hand of the helper with his arm around the lamp-post lead straight to that face with its bulging neck, its flattened ears, its staring eyes and contorted brow, and its open mouth with its thin tongue flapping. Callot often hid the face of the victim; Hogarth never hides it; it was the center of his "pictur'd morals."

And what that face expresses is not simply a momentary pain, though it certainly expresses this. It shows the dog's ineffectual but passionate fight for life. The dog is resisting, as we have noticed, and what he is resisting is the restriction and maiming of his vitality. He is resisting those who would make him a passive sufferer, the slave of their whims. He is a strong dog (the young people in *Marriage* are not unhandsome), and he is accustomed to his own way of moving, his own way of satisfying his needs. In his futile resistance the pain is only one thing that he is fighting—it is a symptom or a part of what he is fighting for, his whole life, power over his own body. In short, he is fighting for freedom, fighting to get away. He is fighting for *his* life.

The Four Stages of Cruelty has essentially only two phases: the first is the maiming and destruction of animals (except for that boy caught under the wheels of the beer-cart in the second engraving); the second is the maiming and destruction of human beings. In the first two plates Nero, though he has taken to hurting larger creatures, has not yet reached the heights of cruelty; he has not yet maimed human beings. But in the next two plates people are maimed; the faces of the victims are the faces of human beings. In these last two plates Hogarth's pictured threat becomes: cruelty to animals moves smoothly into cruelty to human beings, and this in turn moves smoothly into your own destruction. And the last phrase is his weightiest threat: victimize, and you will be victimized. Maim and destroy life and you will be maimed and destroyed. He could not have made that threat if he had kept Nero in the first two stages; there was no capital punishment for mutilating animals. In order to make his threat weighty, he had to move into the realm of cruelty to human beings, and in doing this he entered the realm of horror.

In our chapter on the Gothic Tale we shall come back to the nature of horror. But in these plates it involves not only the slow destruction of a human being; it also involves *larger powers*, more indefinite, more mysterious powers than those involved in, say, a murder mystery. The powers at work in horror tales are not everyday powers; they are unusual, indefinite, larger and darker than life. Nighttime and death are two of the main elements in horror, and they are indefinite to ordinary mortals, often full of fear for us.

It is these larger, indefinite powers that are expressed in the third plate. Tom Nero has killed his trusting sweetheart Ann Gill. He has made her steal from her mistress against her con-

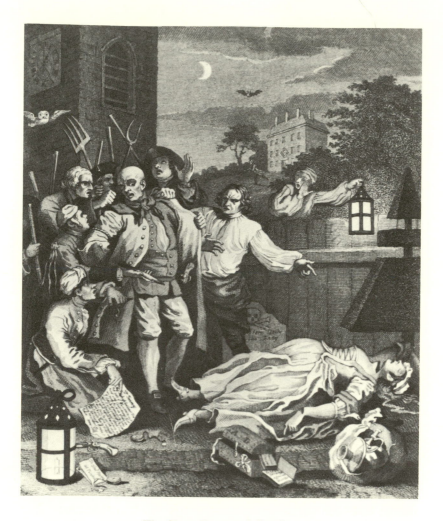

The Four Stages of Cruelty
Cruelty in Perfection

science ("my conscience flies in my face" her note says), and then has ultimately victimized her by knifing her to death. But he has not succeeded in isolating Ann within the circle of his power, and he is himself invaded by the power of society, as well as by the power of darkness and death. The bat, the owl, the dark clouds surrounding the moon, the dark clock tower, the skull and crossbones on the tombstone, the heavenward gaze of the man behind Nero's left shoulder all express indefinite, extraordinary power, and Tom Nero is now trapped in the circle of that power.

And the fourth plate makes all this explicit. On a round table in a round room, at the feet of an enthroned Professor of Anatomy, with the hangman's rope still around his neck, and a hook screwed into his skull, he is suffering the ultimate passivity of the victim; he is being dissected, and a dog will eat what he had of a heart. Again the face of the victim is central. Though the victim is presumably dead his grimace on that round table summarizes the suffering, the slow destruction that society has brought to him.

In every plate of the series the power of the victimizer is being restricted, his prison wall is being breached. In the first plate the boy with the tart is doing this; in the second plate the man in the cab noting Nero's number while Nero beats the galled horse is making a hole in the prison wall; in the third plate everything around him is making him passive; and in the fourth plate he has reached his ultimate slavery, death and dismemberment by others. Hogarth believed that the face and fate of the victim had the power to turn the tables on his victimizer. And this was his threat: be cruel to those who are (apparently) weak, and you will in turn be a victim of cruelty.

But if this is true, what about those victimizers in the last two plates? What about the crowd surrounding Nero, and those physicians? Will they in turn be victimized? For Hogarth the public will (by invoking the laws) stop the cycle of victimization.

The Four Stages of Cruelty
The Reward of Cruelty

The state (and science in that last plate) had, as Max Weber later put it, "the monopoly of the legitimate use of physical force."[8] Only the state could decide which kind of victimization was illegitimate and thereby productive of more victimization, and which kind of cruelty was legitimate and therefore terminal, the last act terminating the cycle of cruelty.

Hogarth was a strong friend of prison reform (see his *Baimbridge on Trial for Murder*), but he did not think of the cruelties visited on convicted criminals as protractedly and as sympathetically as he thought of the cruelties visited on the "born losers," those who are weak and who have never been strong. Cruelty to those who had never been cruel, to those animals, to Ann Gill, to the young people in *Marriage*, this is what he was trying to prevent. And he felt that the best way to do this was *in terrorem*, by frightening people into withholding their power to maim.

But deeper than all his threats and all these distinctions is one belief: the waste of life must be prevented. If one can do his best *in terrorem*, by frightening the strong, so be it. They must be shown how precious life is by being shown themselves as victims. Their fear of victimization must be the way we teach them not to victimize others.

Whatever the merits or faults of this retributive-deterrent doctrine of punishment, Hogarth's position is clear: avoid the waste of life by not hurting the weak. Why? Because when you are cruel your power is temporary, deceptive. There is nowhere to hide from the power of your victim.

CROSSING THE CHANNEL

W E have now taken our first step toward a fuller understanding of cruelty than one gets from simply thinking about pain. Cruelty involves a power-relationship between two parties (where we take "power" to mean the speedy overcoming of resistance, in analogy with its definition in physics); one party is active, comparatively powerful, and the other is passive, comparatively powerless. This difference between the two parties is part of a situation, not simply a personality trait or an internal force in each of the parties. And the situation is one of subjugation, constraint: the victim is limited in his movements by the victimizer, and the situation in which the victimizer oppresses him does not help the victim to fight back or escape—on the contrary, that situation contributes to the powerlessness of the victim. The children of those fathers in the first plate of Hogarth's *Marriage* are in a position of dependence, and those animals and people maimed in the *Cruelty* engravings are being held in subjection either by physical force that is free of effective physical resistance (the boy offering Nero the tart is not resisting Nero in a way that hinders Nero) or by mental forces like love (Ann Gill loved Nero, and stole for him).

And so cruelty involves subordination, subjection to a superior power whose will becomes the victim's law. The superior can exert that power absent-mindedly and peacefully, as the fathers were doing in the *Marriage,* or he can exert it viciously, as Nero was doing in the *Cruelty* engravings. But in either case, the power exerted maims and smashes its victim, while it enhances the life of the victimizer, at least for the moment.

34

And this enhancement for Hogarth is temporary; for him, the power situation shifts (or at least he tries to terrorize his readers into thinking that it will shift), and when that situation shifts, the victimizer will in turn become a victim, will in turn be maimed and smashed under a superior force. This superior force will not be simply physical—it will be social; it will not start a new round of cruelties, but will terminate them, just as Nero's cruelties are terminated in the last plate. The power of the weak for Hogarth is not only to turn the tables on the erstwhile strong; it is also to create a terminal act of cruelty that does not produce new victimizers from the ashes of old victims; it stops the whole cycle of destruction.

This then is the image of the complex structure of cruelty we shall be examining in this book. And the center of that image is the relationship of the active to the passive, the powerful to the weak, whereby the weak are agonized unto death in a situation that permits that power-relationship and that agony.

In Hogarth this image takes the shape of the eventual cessation of cruelty through *reciprocity*, the smashing of the powerful ones themselves. In Sade we shall see it taking a different shape: the continuing enhancement of the lives of the powerful ones, the perpetuation of cruelty in an *irreversible* relationship. For Sade, the victimizer will always be a victimizer, always powerful, always smashing what little resistance his victims give; and the victim will always be a victim, always weak, always being smashed, incapable of enlisting any power in his behalf. These two images of cruelty are similar as far as the *moment* of cruelty is concerned; they differ with regard to the *consequences* of cruelty. In studying Sade, we shall therefore enrich our understanding of that moment, and see a different point of view on the consequences of that moment.

But crossing the Channel can be hard. William Hogarth, the painter and engraver who quite simply hated the waste of life he saw around him, is one kind of man, a simple man. But that descendant of the royal house of Bourbon, Donatien-Alphonse-François, Marquis de Sade, is another kind of man. His thought is complex—even problematic: the records are clear that scandal caused his incarceration, not proved crimes. Apparently, his sexual perversions were never fatal for his victims, nor even excessively painful. But in some of his writings he illustrated and defended the infliction of agony unto death—though in other writings he disclaimed ever defending such cruelties. He is complex indeed, compared to William Hogarth, the friend of the weak, the artist of "pictur'd morals." But the line of our study demands that we go to the most profound student of the moment of cruelty and try to penetrate the depths of his aristocratic eyes.

SADE AND THE MUSIC OF PAIN

VERY few men have defended murder as a way of life, but Sade did so. To him, as to other eighteenth-century Frenchmen, "Nature's Voice" was the voice of truth, but he was one of the few thinkers in history whom that voice counselled to indulge in homicide. In one of his few straightforward tracts, *Philosophy in the Bedroom*, he wrote that "Nature's voice . . . incites us to murderous acts,"[1] and a little later in this work published in 1795, after the Reign of Terror, he wrote, "The freest people are they who are most friendly to murder."[2] Nature, Freedom, the great shibboleths of the French Enlightenment and the French Revolution—to Sade these meant the freedom to destroy human life.

Now it is foolhardy to seek consistency in the life and works of Sade—it was one of his key principles to use lies and subterfuges, "precautions" and "mysteries" as he called them;[3] but some of the inconsistencies in his life and works are very revealing indeed. Here was a friend of murder, and yet one day, sitting precariously, because he was an aristocrat, as chairman of a tribunal functioning at the height of the Reign of Terror, he dared to refuse to condemn certain aristocrats to death. Because of this refusal, he was—predictably—accused of *modérantisme*, was arrested, and was himself condemned to death, though he was not executed. Here was one of the most lucid minds of his century, and a defender of human destruction—why did he refuse to destroy?

The answer is simple, and takes us swiftly into the center of his vision; he gave that answer in 1795, two years after he had been toppled from the tribunal of the *Section des Piques*. Here are

37

his words, in the same relatively straightforward work we have been citing:

> . . . get rid forever of the atrocity of capital punishment . . . the law, cold and impersonal, is a total stranger to the passions which are able to justify in man the cruel act of murder. Man receives his impressions from Nature, who is able to forgive him this act; the law, on the contrary, always opposed as it is to Nature and receiving nothing from her, cannot be authorized to permit itself the same extravagances . . . .[4]

In a few words, this is the philosophy of Sade: the only justification for the "cruel act of murder" is "the passions" of an individual; the law, cold and impersonal, has nothing to do with these, and therefore is not justified in killing men. To kill in cold blood is unnatural. Only hot blood can justify murder.

The Marquis de Sade was not a friend of torture and killing for their own sake, or he would have approved of capital punishment. He was a friend of "the passions" for *their* own sake, and the passions he was a friend of were the passions of those he sometimes called the "vigorous spirits" or "powerful beings," those energetic enough, courageous enough to be stimulated by cruelty. He was primarily concerned with *these*, not with victims or their deaths.

Hogarth too in his cruelty engravings was concerned with the Tom Neros of the world, the cruel ones; he too exhibited their powerful passions. But he exhibited them in a "progress" which warned us not to take them as models. Sade exhibited them usually in novels that were intended, like Hogarth's "pictur'd morals," to encourage certain kinds of behavior;[5] but *his* vigorous beings were always exemplars. In fact the most destructive beings in history were exemplars for *them*. Olympia towards the end of Sade's "moralistic" novel *Juliette* says:

> "Incendiary Nero is my model; I too would like to stand on my balcony, a lyre in my hand, and while singing gaze forth upon my native land become a pyre to my countrymen."[6]

Both Sade and Hogarth dealt with clear, particular cases designed to encourage their readers to perform actions of particular sorts, but different sorts.

In his preface to *Philosophy* Sade wrote:

Lewd women, let the voluptuous Saint-Ange be your model;
after her example, be heedless of all that contradicts pleasure's
divine laws. . . .

. . . imitate the fiery Eugénie, be as quick as she to destroy, to
spurn all those ridiculous precepts inculcated in you by imbecile
parents. . . .

. . . study the cynical Dolmancé, proceed like him . . . sacrificing
everything to the senses' pleasures. . . .[7]

But what are the main differences between these two ways
of using powerful, passionate beings as guides for action? There is
no better way to answer this question than by extracting from
behind all those Sadean evasions the core of his doctrine of the
vigorous spirit, the victimizer, as we have been calling him.

The key metaphor of Sade's writing is heat—disorderly energy. His main injunction is: be hot with spontaneous action and
passion, like a sentient volcano; do not be cold under the public
restraints your fellow men try to lay upon you. Follow your
drives no matter what the results are; do not allow anything
outside you (like other people, religion, or law) to restrict them.
Nature as a whole has nothing outside herself to restrict her—no
God, no concern for beings outside herself. She has her physical
laws, but these are internal, the blood streams of her vitality, not
the chains of enslavement. Something in man wants bleak order-
liness in society at large and in the bodies of its particular members—and this something creates customs and laws, and tempts
some men to kiss their chains while they slowly die of boredom.
But nature in the raw makes each creature hunger for the bodies
of other living creatures without compassion and without a timid
desire for peace. As decadent, Christianized animals, our highest
duty and privilege is to be utterly unrestrained, like Vesuvius
swallowing Pompeii or a lion pushing his nose and mouth into
the warm flesh of a freshly killed deer.

Through all of his literary and philosophical devices this

exhortation bursts: Boil! Go! Keep the heat of excitement alive in yourself by acting cruelly and heedlessly, not kindly and fearfully. Stay hot with heedless passion.

In the process of defending a boiling life and attacking death in life, two major directions developed in his thought: one centripetal, and the other centrifugal. In that long philosophical novel *Aline et Valcour* he has Sarmiento, one of his large brotherhood of immensely energetic heroes, use a crucial term to summarize one of these directions: *"l'isolisme."* Isolation simply means that a man feels only in his flesh; his nerve-ends terminate at his skin. Incidentally, this isolationism has nothing to do with philosophic positions like solipsism or subjectivism: all his heroes believe with him in an external physical world whose existence is as sure as the existence of their own need to hurt. Their kind of isolationism is the denial of compassion, and the celebration of the fire in their own flesh.

But there can be no fire without friction, and so the second direction of Sade's thought is outward, toward violent collision. The power of a Sadean hero is quite simply his power to smash others. And the only heat he knows is the heat generated in that smashing. In all his major works Sade says essentially the same thing: man is an intricately ordered chunk of matter ("an absolutely material plant," as Noirceuil puts it in *Juliette*) whose usual pleasures are nothing but harmonious, peaceful movements of "molecules." But Noirceuil, Sarmiento, Juliette, and Sade himself are what he often describes as "blasé," have had enough of these calm movements. Only when impressions strike a man crookedly and do not blend with his own organic molecules can he come alive, come aware. Such a person develops a taste for irritation, for the impact of things upon his nervous system. Simple pleasure no longer arouses him because its objects blend or fuse with his own flesh and feelings. Shock, the impact of objects that do not blend with his body but repel it and shake it, shock is what the powerful, blasé individual requires.

Sade had drawn his vocabulary from D'Holbach's and La Mettrie's materialism, but he extended their meaning beyond their rather peaceful, bourgeois ethics. Collision for Sade had two sorts of targets: society as a whole, and particular victims. Society with all of its devices for keeping us cool and orderly had itself to be shocked, scandalized, and hopefully blown up (as we noticed, Sade sometimes contemplated a world of Sadeans doing what his heroes did, smashing custom, law, peace, and bringing disorderly energy, great heat, vitality into the world at last). He wanted to feel the poignant sensation of smashing the invisible but real flesh and bone of society. The sound of public protest and the feeling that he was violating public patterns were, as he put it, "a whiplash to my nerves."

But his main target was not society in general; it was juicy victims, particular living flesh. In the end what he and his libertines wanted was erotic stimulation. The screams and blood of a victim, these were what stirred their "life principle" most directly. They could have an orgasm best when they were making somebody (even themselves) suffer substantially. Algolagnia, the pleasure that pain can be or bring, is the key concept of Sade's life and works. The joy he got in this actual fleshly collision was what he once called the "irrational extravagance" he spent much of his adult life turning into a rational philosophy.

His description of the frontispiece to a poem entitled "The Truth" summarizes his way of keeping alive. The motto under the picture is a line from the poem: "Delivering ourselves up ceaselessly to our most monstrous drives," and the picture itself shows, according to his description,

> A handsome young man naked, with his penis in the ass of a girl who is also naked. With one hand he is seizing her by the hair and turning her face towards his, and with the other he is ramming a dagger into her bosom. Under their feet are the three persons of the Trinity . . . . Above, Nature, in glory, with a crown of flowers.[8]

The solitary pleasure of collision with flesh keeps his "life principle" boiling.

In *Juliette*, Saint-Fond, one of Sade's vigorous spirits, summarizes both the sensual isolation and the sensual collision that are central to Sade's thought

> . . . shared, all enjoyment becomes dilute, the wine becomes watered . . . there is no more selfish passion than lust; none that is severer in its demands; 'tis with yourself you must be solely concerned,

and as for the object that serves you, it must always be considered as some sort of victim, destined to that passion's fury. Do not all passions require victims?[9]

The mechanism whereby victimizing stimulates vitality was simple for Sade: the sight or thought of the pain of others stirs up our "animal spirits," which transmit a disturbance to our bowels, and arouse us sexually even though we may be tired or bored at the outset.

Now irritation (and therefore stimulation) is maximized when fleshly and verbal collisions are brought together; words and deeds "irritate the electrical particles of your neural humour" as Juliette says to the Countess de Donis. Every thought that is "unusual" or "aberrant" irritates and stimulates even the most blasé mind. Customary or conventional morality may be boring when simply expressed, because it is so usual; but when that morality is flatly violated in thought as well as action, the result is the greater enhancement of our vitality, the more intense warming up of our energies. And this is why the writings of Sade are full of criminal thoughts. At one point in her story Juliette whispers to another vigorous spirit, "A criminal thought excites most wondrously, does it not?"[10]

For Sade the only freedom one can have is the freedom of the energetic person to desire and do more than the feeble ones. For him there is no freedom from causes of a physiological and psychological sort; each of us is "the toy of natural influences" as Juliette puts it.[11] The only freedom is the freedom of the energetic libertines who are still "the toy of natural influences" but who need and do more than the feeble ones, and are therefore freer from convention and laws than weak ones. And energy is stimulated by irritation, one speaks *and* does what is unusual, irritating, confusing. His most active protagonists often say things like "let us now turn to perpetrating some of this delicious evil in order to keep the habit bright . . . "[12] and their interlocutors reply with remarks like "by all means . . . but this projected evil, in order that it delight us the more, let us perpetrate it thoughtfully."

This is why paradox—or perverseness—is everywhere to be found in Sade—he is always asking us to deliver ourselves up "ceaselessly to our most monstrous drives" because words like "monstrous" usually involve something to be *avoided*. His writing and his doing what is contrary to general opinion are done in order to unclog and stimulate our energies. Thinking perversely and acting viciously are Sade's two aphrodisiacs.

Sade wanted isolation and collision—but are the two really compatible with each other? When you collide with society and individuals, does it make any sense to say you are isolated from them? Of course, one can reconcile them by saying that Sade wants us to be stimulated by the feelings or reactions of others, not restrained by them. He wants us to be isolated in the sense of not being restrained by others, and he wants us to collide in the sense of being stimulated by others.

But consider this case of a real collision between Sade himself and society: he is sitting in his prison cell for all those years with his terrible headaches, his spells of dizziness, his bleeding nose, his yearning for space in which to move. Here is a part of a letter he writes:

> Even if I had been the lowest individual on earth they would hardly have ventured on the barbarous treatment of which I was made the victim; in a word, I have lost my sight, my lungs have been ruined and through lack of exercise I have become so monstrously corpulent that I can hardly stir; . . . I have no longer any taste or love for anything . . . .[13]

The question arises: when we collide with others, can we keep them from restraining us? Can we attack society and individuals with impunity? Is it always stimulating and life-enhancing to do violence? This passage, and most of Sade's correspondence from prison, seem to indicate that the answer in all cases is negative: it takes two to collide, and the *other* may not simply stimulate you; he may smash *you*, as Sade found out over the course of his whole adult life (he spent twenty-eight years in prisons and asylums), and as Hogarth insisted in his engravings.

To begin to see how he solves this problem, consider the

examples of libertines that he presents to us in his main novels. For instance in *The 120 Days of Sodom* his libertines operate in

> ... a remote and isolated retreat, as if silence, distance, and stillness were libertinage's patent vehicles ...

Silling, where the libertines spent their 120 days, is in the Black Forest, on the far side of great obstacles. He dreams up a hundred devices for keeping the heroes free of all resistance. As a small part of his description of the approach to Silling, he writes:

> Having passed the village, you began to scale a mountain almost as high as the Saint Bernard and infinitely more difficult to climb, for the only way to reach the summit is by foot ... Five long hours are needed to reach the peak of the mountain, and there you come upon another extraordinary feature which, owing to the precautions that had been taken, became a new barrier so insurmountable that none but birds might overcome it; the topographical accident we refer to is a crevice above sixty yards wide which splits the crest into northern and southern parts, with the result that, after having climbed up the mountain, it is impossible, without the aid of great skill, to go back down it. Durcet had united these two parts, between which a precipice fell to the depth of above a thousand feet, by a fine wooden bridge which was retired immediately the last of the crew had arrived, and from this moment on, all possibility of communication with the Castle of Silling ceased.[14]

In all of Sade's works, literary creations like these keep his libertines at liberty to crush their particular victims with impunity. In *Juliette*, vast wealth, friends in high positions, dungeon walls, and amazing good luck keep the heroine and her fellow club members from any confrontation with mobs, the law, or the relatives of the victims. Neatly isolated within these devices they cut and gouge and screw and smash to their heart's content, with no resistance, and with just enough awareness of their own wrongdoing to give poignancy to their pleasure.

But what about the resistance of the victims themselves, as fleshly individuals? In all of his works except *Justine* the victim is stylized out of all particularity and force. She indulges in graceful writhings with her *éblouissante* skin and her undulating auburn hair; she is forever throwing herself at the knees of the victimizer—and if that can't excite him into taking one more good chunk out of her, what would? She uses empty, flowery, archaic language while she is hugging his stiff knees, her head presumably nestling comfortably against his penis, and she offers no solid resistance at all. Well, in *Aline et Valcour*, Léonore while being raped shows *him:* she just lies there and doesn't let herself get sexually excited at all!

With all those compliant but titillating victims surrounded by a silent, inefficacious society, the Sadism of Sade is much like Juliette's orgiastic club-meetings, where people agree to maltreat each other and to be maltreated in turn, but nobody puts up any resistance because nobody is really getting hurt. Of course non-members get destroyed, but they are as graceful and titillating in their fall as a feather brushed down a naked foot. The emblem of all this for me is a certain scene in *Juliette* where the heroine says in a playful society-voice to her female companion, "Come now, darling, let's pop into bed and do something *execrable* to each other!" And her friend gaily calls out, "Oh, *let's!*" Sade does not see the humor in the scene because all of his victims are about as compliant as this one.

Occasionally, especially in *Justine*, we experience the victim's pain, sometimes quite movingly expressed; but that pain is an island that never resists the victimizer's passion. The pain helps *stimulate* his passion. Pain is the most passive reaction to harm, if we think of these reactions as making a spectrum from painful writhing through angry glaring to vengeful acting. We experience pain on our backs, anger while we are arising, and vengeance on our feet. Sade's victims are forever on their backs. Justine, for instance, is always amazed by the harm that comes to her, by the new knife-slashes or buggerings or perfidies, amazed, but seldom or never really angry, let alone vengeful. Sometimes she shows hints of a desire to call in public authorities, but Sade arranges the libertinage of her victimizers in exactly the way he arranges the libertinage of *The 120 Days* and of all his other writings. Her more powerfully reactive or active feelings die aborning, die of inefficacy in a Sadean world where victims have only a passive role to play, like puppets.

Madame de Clairvil puts it neatly in *Juliette* when she praises torturing "some youthful object, appealing and mild"; she says that it is emphatically voluptuous

> . . . to be amused by her tears, excited by her distress, irritated by her capers, inflamed by her writhings, by that voluptuous dancing performed to the music of pain. . . .

And she goes on to describe how stimulating are "the contortions of sufferings and the twitching caused by despair."[15] For Sade's libertines there is no collision between human beings, there is only titillation. The music of pain produces a voluptuous dance for which the victimizer has written the score and arranged the performance. There is as little danger of his victim being angry, let alone vengeful, as there is danger that a ballerina will leap off the stage and throttle the conductor or a member of the audience. Pain like music holds the "dancer" in his role and helps make the whole spectacle titillating.

There is a story told in *The Theory and Practice of Hell* by Eugene Kogon about a dancer standing naked in line waiting for her execution in the concentration camp. A guard tells her to step out of line and dance. She does, and carried away with her own authoritative action and with her individuality she dances up to the guard, takes his gun, and shoots him. This sort of dance never occurs in Sade. The music of pain renders the victim passive, *enthralled*.

Let us look at this whole matter of the victimizer's impunity from another point of view—consequences. In Sade's novels the libertines suffer no painful consequences from their libertinage. On the contrary, they do nothing but thrive from moment to moment. This is the whole point of the novels *Justine* and *Juliette*. Consequences are never a resistance or force. Juliette the cruel, evil one goes from glory to glory. Once when she is in danger of suffering vengeance, she simply adds a little note to a letter delivered by her would-be victimizers, a note to the effect: come and save me! And of course she is saved! This is one of the very rare instances wherein consequences even exist as a force to collide with in the works of Sade. In the vast majority of examples, not only are there no social consequences in the sense of social vengeance for cruel deeds, there are no personal consequences: victims do not retaliate, and even one's own body shows no effects of libertinage. Juliette lives from fresh moment to fresh moment, her body as blooming as ever, even after all those debauches.

Impunity from consequences is nowhere more neatly emblematized than in the virginal "ointment" Juliette employs early in her career. Juliette has just been deflowered and she asks her mentor

> "My best beloved, however shall you repair all the damage that's just been done?" . . . Delbène made me answer; "tomorrow, I'll massage you with an ointment that so wonderfully restores their whole order to things that afterwards no one would ever guess they'd been exposed to rude usage."[16]

Later in *Juliette* we learn that the ointment is

> . . . an extract of myrtle, rub yourself with it in the morning and before retiring at night, nine days of that ought to suffice. On the tenth you'll find yourself as much a virgin as you were emerging from the womb of your mother."[17]

In the intimacy of the victimizers' bodies, as in their social and personal relationships, there is in Sade's writings no struggle with consequences.

In all the editions of his two most famous novels, *Justine* and *Juliette*, as in his other works, the absence of such consequences, the absence of collision with resistance is Sade's great "argument" for libertinage. The victory of the strong over all adversity carries with it for Sade great persuasive force. Sade knew that both his libertines and his readers would be cooled off by real resistance. As Saint-Fond says to Juliette:

> . . . obstacles, exerting their restrictive influence upon the form of your delirium, will always tend to confine it within the boundaries of decency and virtue, thus altering its essence; upon your delirium obstacles of any sort have a dampening effect, water poured on fire; a hindering effect, so many chains, so many clogs . . . .[18]

In all these ways Sade succeeds in avoiding real collision in his novels and writings, the collision of two active forces, the victimizer's and his victim's. It is plain that whatever resistance Sade admits is a caress, not a fist in the face—a spark, not a pail of water. To return to his basic metaphor of heat, he arranges things so that the victimizer's energy is always being warmed, and never being dampened.

At this point it is important to see the difference between Sadism, as it occurs in Sade's novels, and Masochism, as it occurs in the novels of Leopold von Sacher-Masoch. If Sade were saying the same thing as Masoch, then the absence of resistance from his victims would be more easily understandable. Masoch's *Venus in Furs* is the story of a man's active, aggressive desire to be victimized: the masochist Severin corrupts the sexually normal Wanda into what she calls a "game" of furs and whips and degradation; he, Severin, creates the whole game and drags her into the masochistic relationship that pains and humiliates and pleases him. In Masoch's novels there is understandably only a token resistance from the "victim," only enough reaction and action from him to make his own pleasure-pain complete. In his world there is no totally victimized victim—all victims are very much accomplices, compliant—in fact, *they* are the powerful ones.

But Sade is another matter. For instance, in *Juliette*, that eloquent spokesman for Sadism, Noirceuil, places himself in the center of a circle made by two naked boys, his naked wife, and Juliette, also naked; they are getting ready for their next orgy, and Noirceuil's modest wife asks him if he derives his pleasure in these matters from her despair; Noirceuil answers:

> "I do, Madame, and in significant measure . . . believe me when I affirm that my enjoyment would be far less were you any more willing to comply with it."[19]

In almost all of his works (with the exception of the first parts of *Philosophy in the Bedroom*, which is an orgy where nobody is being substantially hurt) the victim does not create the game and set the rules. Justine is always being raped, violated, forced; every orgy she enters, she enters on the victimizer's terms, not her own. The rules are not her rules, the action is not initiated by her will.

Those (like Sartre) who believe Sadism is essentially the same as Masochism have not looked carefully at the victims the two novelists portray. Sade's victims are not accomplices; Masoch's "victims" are accomplices—or rather, to put it more accurately, are their own oppressors. The "jolt" or collision Sade demands to set his "animal spirits" boiling requires a totally unwilling victim. For Sadism only real cruelty, substantial harm, and usually death, can make those vital juices *boil*.

The following dialogue summarizes the all-important differences between the two kinds of victimization:

Masochist: Hurt me.
Sadist: No.

There must be a collision of will as well as body for Sade; the collision is muffled by obvious compliance for Masoch. We have treated Sade at length and not Masoch, because only such a collision of mind and body can be plainly called "cruelty." When there is obvious instigation and *no conceivable* resistance on the part of the victim, the word "cruelty" has been radically altered in its meaning, altered even beyond our broad use of that word.

Sade sought to exemplify real cruelty, but did so without allowing the victim to offer real resistance to the victimizer. He wanted only to exhibit the titillation of the victimizer at a given moment, and he wrote his novels accordingly.

What all of these devices amount to is a celebration of contemporaneity, of the now, at least for the victimizer. The sensation of the moment, the felt heat of mild irritation happening now is the locus of all Sade's examples. This is why his works are so episodic, one thing after another, with only the thinnest excuse for a plot or mathematical plan (as in *The 120 Days*) to hold the episodes together. His novels, and all his writings, are made up of separate present moments.

All of his exemplary novels and dialogues have the following form, or something very much resembling it: demonstration, then dissertation, then demonstration, then dissertation. That is, and here I am using the particular language of his *Philosophy in the Bedroom*, first there is a demonstration or particular action involving victimization; then there is a dissertation on the justification or analysis of the action; then there is another demonstration. There is this sort of alternation in some of Hogarth's progresses, especially the *Marriage:* stressed plate, unstressed plate, stressed plate, and so on. In the stressed or active plate the sharp distinction between victim and victimizer is central, while in the unstressed plates of comparative inaction or passivity there is no such sharp distinction between the stronger and the weaker.

The same holds for Sade's writings. In the dissertations, the victim can (mildly) talk back, can expostulate a little (very little indeed), and not force but persuasion is being used. But persuasion does not involve the victim-victimizer relationship. It is colloquy, not violence. The demonstrations, however, are pure violence.

But when Sade's libertines animadvert on cruelty and try to convert their victims or each other to the creed of the Sadistic Moment, Sade is not giving up his basic love of the moment in favor of abstract, systematic logic or metaphysics. There is a self-contradictory logic and metaphysics to Sade's various dissertations, but we understand him ill if we try to understand him as a disinterested system-builder.

The dissertations come after the orgasms and provide their own momentary titillation, while the participants in the orgy are recovering their physical powers. Immense as their powers are they have to be recuperated, and so there is talk. Talk is delightful not only to help pass the time of recuperation, but for its own sake—"manipulating your metaphysics prettily" (as Saint-Fond puts it in *Juliette*)[20] is full of delight for Sade and for his libertines. As Sade puts it in *Juliette,*

> Delbène finally screamed, ... "Enough, 'tis done ... let's sit down now, let's talk a bit ... There's more to it than just experiencing sensations, they must also be analyzed. Sometimes it is as pleasant to discuss as to undergo them; and when one has reached the limit of one's physical means, one may then exploit one's intellect.[21]

It is important to see that Sade, like La Rochefoucauld, Montaigne, and so many other thinkers, was a moment-centered, epigrammatic writer at least as much as he was a frustrated systematic thinker. The contradictions that zealous, pedantic commentators have found in his writings, and even within a given speech by the same character in the same situation, these contradictions are hob-goblins only for systematic minds. Sade had a lucid and ever-awake intelligence; I am certain that the contradictions to be found in his writings did not escape him—they simply did not concern him. An idea for him was a moment of excitement primarily. Vague relations between ideas sometimes seemed to have interested him—but it was each idea that he delectated most, not a consistent system of them, and the sudden pleasant shock of uttering an anti-public, anti-religious, anti-moral idea was its own best excuse for being. Realizing this, I have not played the easy game of collating contradictions in his writing. Such collations are irrelevant to what he wanted to do. He wanted to offer excitement of a verbal or conceptual sort in alternation with excitement of a quasi-visual, descriptive sort (during his "demonstrations"). "Excitement *now*" was his motto, not "systems forever."

In fact, toward the end of *Juliette* Sade leads us to believe that at least as much as trying to change the world, his writings are efforts to excite himself. As a matter of fact, he wrote his works almost entirely while incarcerated, away from the actual orgies he yearned for. Those twenty-eight years were twenty-eight years of dissertations. Of course, questions of intent in an artist, especially one committed in principle to public deceit for self-preservation's sake, are very knotty and difficult ones to answer definitively. And so let us not say that self-titillation was the only motive for Sade's writing all those many formal works he wrote in various prisons and asylums under various types of conditions, including severe physical restriction.

But anyone trying to get a full picture of Sade's world should read the following passage: Juliette is talking with the Countess de Donis about those situations when one's desires exceed one's means for satisfying them (and of course Sade's imprisonment was such a situation). Juliette is telling the Countess how to "aggravate your sensations" so as to keep excited and to keep from being bored:

> Go a whole fortnight without lewd occupations, divert yourself, amuse yourself at other things ... At the close of the final day retire alone to your bed, calmly and in silence; lying there, summon up all those images and ideas you have banished during the fasting

period just elapsed, and indolently, languidly, nonchalantly fall to performing that wanton little pollution by which nobody so cunningly arouses herself or others as you. Next, unpent your fancy, let it freely dwell upon aberrations of different sorts and of ascending magnitude; linger over the details of each, pass them all one by one in review; assure yourself that you are sovereign absolute in a world grovelling at your feet. Fear of reprisals, hindrances you have none: choose what pleases you, but leave nothing out, make no exceptions; show consideration to no one whomsoever, sever every hobbling tie, abolish every check, let nothing stand in your way; leave everything to your imagination, let it pursue its bent and content yourself to follow in its train . . . Without your noticing it, from among all the various scenes you visualize one will claim your attention more energetically than the others, and will so forcefully rivet itself in your mind that you'll be unable to dislodge it or supplant it by another. Once this is accomplished, light your bedside lamp and write out a full description of the abomination which has just inflamed you . . .[22]

And so she goes on to tell her interlocutor how to write a Sadean novel.

To a very great extent, the key "faculty" or aspect of consciousness for Sade is the imagination, the fancy that combines and recombines words and images and feelings.

His fullest discussion of the imagination occurs in *Philosophy in the Bedroom*. The imagination is formed in us substantially by our physiological inheritance, but it can operate at its best only when the mind is "absolutely free of prejudices," as Madame de Saint-Ange puts it. When the superficial obstacles of conventional timidity are exploded, it can operate; but even one of the prejudices or fears that society foists on us will suffice to "chill" the imagination. For Sade the imagination is "the mainspring of everything," the source of our most piquant delights. It is disorderly, proceeds in passionate outbursts not systems, and indeed as Madame Saint-Ange says, " . . . of all regularity . . . it is an enemy, it worships disorder . . . ."[23]

When we see the importance in his thought of a heated,

energetic, capricious imagination we begin to understand how a philosophy of the insulated Now can make sense. In our imaginations, not in our daily experiences or the insipid moral precepts of society, we can in esthetic safety invent our ointments against consequences and watch people dance to the music of pain. In imagination, if not in reality, we can find collision, but not real collision—we can find imaginary, fanciful collision. Because our imagination is limited only by its own powers and not by outward objects, we can regulate these collisions so that they become esthetic contemplations of a dance, ticklings, pleasurable irritations, harmless, autonomous excitements.

In Sade's concept of imagination, vague and ambiguous as it is, everything that has been said in this chapter is explained. Sade is speaking from and to the imagination when he offers his examples, and so he can imagine away all resistance to the momentary caprices of his vigorous beings. When he sees pain as music, and agonized writhing as the dance to that music, he does so by virtue of his imagination, which can, like music and dance themselves, isolate us from ordinary experience and can create disorder with impunity.

And so we have answered the question concerning the relationship between isolation and collision in his thought. Collision is always circumscribed by man's (especially the strong being's) isolation. It occurs in his novels not as a dampening or destructive conflict with the external world, but as an imagined irritation that excites Sade into energetic enjoyment.

Sade condones cruelty by making the victimizers virtually innocent: their victims are so passive, so stylized, so much like what Hegel called the "zero" of the slave in the master-slave relationship, that the cruel ones seem to be maiming or killing *no one*. There is a kind of innocence to his way of treating cruelty. Isolated moments, isolated victimizers, that is, moments and victimizers isolated from all destructively inimical forces, these constitute the imaginative vision of Sade.

But for Hogarth, as our analysis of the *Marriage* and the *Cruelty* engravings indicates, there is no such thing as impunity for victimizers. The power of the victim and of the society that surrounds him and the very nature of the cause-effect relationship can work against him. (If you hurt smaller animals you grow into hurting bigger and more resistant animals, and these animals, especially if they are people, have greater strength to hurt you than do the little, more expendable ones.) It is not simply the continuity of time in the form of progresses that makes Hogarth differ from Sade as far as cruelty is concerned, not only the power and individuality of the weak to "dampen" the fires of the victimizer; it is basically a belief in the reality of the cause-effect relationship in such matters that is the difference between their views of cruelty. Hogarth believed in a causal law that might be called "Reciprocity": what you do unto others they (or someone) may well somehow manage to do unto you. And he also believed in the power, within the given moment of cruelty, of the victim's particular face and reactions to dampen the excitement of the viewer. These two beliefs are basic components, as we have seen, of an Hogarthian attitude towards cruelty and victimization in general.

Though he obviously selected or invented progresses to suit his purposes, Hogarth believed in a common-sense world wherein you are exposed to resistance as much as your victims are exposed to resistance. He was confident, and he felt that his audience was confident, that this was the case. Sade believed in a world radically unlike the world of his own personal experience: a world veiled in impunity for the victimizer. His own imprisonment showed him how imaginary this world was, and he did not try to make it a plausible or common-sensical world. He tried only to make it exciting, not boring, imaginatively stimulating for himself and for his libertines.

One can sum up the difference by saying that for Hogarth the face of the victim was a powerful force in a given moment and a force whose ruination could bring ruination upon the ruiner; for Sade the face of the victim was an imaginative construction outside of the causal laws. It could not act as a resistant force either on the spectator or on the libertine. Sade's victims do not have individual ways of acting *vis-à-vis* their victimizers; they have only pain, which is, as we have noticed, one element of the life of the victim. And lacking resistant power, having only the power to suffer, they are not solid forces in the world. By emphasizing only the passive element in the life of the victim, Sade makes even Justine a product of the imagination, not a real force in the world.

A Brief Descent into Fundamentals

Let us make our distinctions between Hogarthian and Sadean attitudes towards cruelty more fundamental. They are different attitudes towards reality, and we should, however briefly, see them as such.

The men we usually call "Existentialists" (Kierkegaard, Nietzsche, Sartre and others) believe that human existence is fullest when the individual is isolated from and in conflict with the "Public Thing" or *Res Publica*. Kierkegaard's enemy was "the universal," the secular and religious laws or abstractions that make a man not a passionately *deciding*, spiritual being, but a passionlessly *conforming*, cog-like being, incapable of deep feeling, incapable of his own spiritual or moral choices. And for Kierkegaard[24] paradox, contradiction, releases minds from neat, orderly, publicly persuasive arguments, and frees us for passionate, isolated decision-making. It is this special kind of isolation that the person in Kierkegaard's highest stage of existence, the Religious Stage, has, this special kind of riskful choice and fear and trembling, that have made modern Existentialists so interested in Sade. For Sade too sought autonomy from the Republic, from the universal laws of morality, politics, and religion; Sade too wanted to make decisions for himself. Sade too used paradox, or apparent contradictions, conflicts to help break the hold on the individual of common-sense and common morality, etc. Kierkegaard and Sade, for all their differences as far as sexual eroticism and the victimization of others are concerned, both believed that a passionate, anti-establishment individual is more fully alive than a conforming, calm, comfortable individual.

Nietzsche expressed his individualism by deploring "the herd" and praising the *Übermensch*, and Sartre celebrates the man who does not fall into "bad faith" by playing roles and thinking of himself as a thing with no other being but a public function. But however various Existentialists express it, individualism by way of collision with public authority (and its right hand, common sense), is important to the mainstream of their writings. Isolation through conflict, individualism through passionate rebellion and paradox, these are what the Existentialists —and Sade—defended.

But equally important for relating Sade to philosophers who were more careful than he was in developing their positions is the Existentialist notion of The Moment, The Now, or what Kierkegaard in all his main works (most plainly perhaps in *Training in Christianity*) called "contemporaneity." For Kierkegaard, when one is fully alive, fully existent, fully aware, "there is only one tense: the present" (as he puts it in the section "Christianity as the Absolute" in *Training*). For him, Christ, full of paradox as he is (being both eternal and temporal, God and man, omnipotent and a victim) occurs in the *present* for us or he does not occur at all in any real sense. He says in the same section of *Training*:

> ... what really occurred [the past] is not ... the real. It lacks the determinant which is the determinant of truth [as inwardness] ... The past is not reality—for me ... only the contemporary is reality for me ... for Christ's life on earth, sacred history stands for itself alone outside history.[25]

And this is the heart of Sade's similarity with the Existentialists: they are "outside history" when it comes to having full existence. Throughout his works Kierkegaard denies that antecedents or consequences have anything to do with belief in Jesus or with a full existence. In *Training*, for example, Kierkegaard says that we can never existentially "know" Jesus by the consequences of his actions, by the history of Christianity. From "history we can learn to know nothing about Him,"[26] he says; only by experiencing his life and passion as contemporary with our own lives, as *now*, can we achieve full existence.

This isolation from history and from public authority has often been called (sometimes by Existentialists) "subjectivity." But whatever philosophic terms we use, it is useful to see Sade's kind of advocacy of isolation and collision as closer to some of the Existentialists than to any other modern philosophies.

On the other hand, the emphasis on the individual's own present moment is of course not at all characteristic of Hogarth's engravings. The progresses of Hogarth are, profoundly, histories. The past influences the present importantly, and the present has its important consequences. Hogarth's victims and victimizers are by no means isolated from the public weal. His morality is not only consistent with that welfare, but is meant to enhance it: the preservation of life that he sought is as much the preservation of public orderly life as it is the preservation of individuals.

Moreover, interaction between victims and victimizers, and between both and the rest of society, are the rule in Hogarth's engravings. The victims, as we have often said, exert a momentous force on the victimizers, and society exerts a great force on both. These interactions are an assumption of Hogarth that operates powerfully in every progress he ever drew.

If one would place him in a philosophic tradition, it would have to be a tradition that goes from Locke and the British Empiricists to modern Pragmatists. John Locke in his *Essay Concerning Human Understanding* emphasized an "historical plain method" for attaining knowledge of all things. Facts for him had consequences that we must understand if we would believe what we should believe. Locke, the practical physician and quondam public servant, founded our knowledge on man's sense-relationship with his external world. And the modern Pragmatists, especially John Dewey, celebrate always the active and reactive, "doing and undergoing" relationship between man and his environment, man and his society, man and the objects and persons around him. For a Pragmatist like Dewey, history is of the essence, and the now is an incident, involved on both sides in causes and effects. To understand a man (or anything else) for a Deweyan Pragmatist is to understand a history of interaction with other things. Dewey's world is a world of progresses, of real struggles, of real encounters with nature and with other persons.

It is a world where scientific laws have great relevance, and a world where individual psychology, sociology, and political science make a seamless whole, with no sharp breaks between the individual and other individuals, or between the individual and society at large. In fact, in a Deweyan world, there are no sharp breaks at all—all is continuity, a dynamic continuity of interactions. Consequently isolation is non-existent, and collision becomes the real collision of organisms with an environment, not the internalized collision of paradox. With the Pragmatists, as with Hogarth, we are back in history with its struggles and its events leading to other events. We are back in the everyday and the scientific world, not of subjectivity, but of publicly observable action. It is a world where passion is secondary to action and interaction, the mirror image of a world where action is secondary to passion or to inward awareness.

Of course there are exceptions to the generalization that has just been drawn; but it is a useful one nonetheless. Sade's view of violence and cruelty has its roots in the kind of isolation and collision that the Existentialists analyzed; Hogarth's view of violence and cruelty has its roots in the real, forcible collision that Dewey and other Pragmatists analyzed. Anybody who wants to make a judgment between these two views of cruelty must see how fundamental the differences between them are if he would make a circumspect judgment.

It is not enough to say that Hogarth saw the power of the weak on the strong, and Sade did not see the face and force of the victim. We are here confronted with two powerful and different views of reality.

Back to the Surface

But this is all rather abstract for a discussion that makes much of example, of particular cases located in particular places at particular times.

If one would put Sade in perspective as far as examples are concerned, one should compare him with another novelist, not with philosophers whom I suspect he despised and whom he used only in order to make his examples and novels more exciting. Nor should we compare him only to a painter like Hogarth.

Instead of making another abstract comparison of Sade with other writers, I should like to quote a few passages from a novelist who did see the victim as active, as having a way of life, not simply a passive moment of pain. Louis-Ferdinand Céline, despite his personal advocacy in his later years of massacring Jews, was in his main novels just such a pragmatist-novelist. His description of the power of the weak was one of his greatest contributions to world literature.

In *Journey to the End of the Night* there is a scene wherein a drunken, ordinarily impotent couple terrorize all the weak creatures in their house in order to get excited enough to have sex up against the kitchen sink. Céline describes carefully how they stamp hard on the dog's paw, and laugh wildly while it runs howling under the bed "like a soul in torment." But Céline keeps his most detailed descriptions for their victimization of their little girl:

> The little girl was needed first; they called her in. She knew. She started whimpering at once. She knew what was going to happen to her. Judging by her voice, she must have been about ten years old. . . .They must have been tying her to the bedposts. All this time the child was whimpering like a mouse in a trap. 'Oh, no, you won't escape, I tell you, . . . ' the woman went on, and a stream of imprecations followed as if she were talking to a horse. . . . 'Be quiet, Mamma!' the little girl answered softly. 'Be quiet, Mamma! Whack me—but don't talk like that, Mamma! . . .'[27]

The style of that girl leaps forth from the passage. Sade would be content with only her pain (her whimpering like a mouse in a trap), but her reaction as a force in her own right interests Céline.

In the following passage he describes the passive suffering of the animal, but in a way that makes the animal, even though it is only passive, real in a way that reminds us vaguely of Sade's description of Justine's suffering (though even in *Justine* Sade always transmuted her sufferings into the excitement and pleasure of her victimizers). This passage from Céline's *Journey* reminds one of Hogarth's compassion for the weak, and specifically of the second plate of Hogarth's *Cruelty* engravings:

Personally, I should have been glad to throw Major Pinçon to the sharks, and his policemen [who had been persecuting the common soldiers] with him . . . just to teach them the proper way to live.

And my horse could have gone too, so that he shouldn't suffer any more. He hadn't any back left, poor brute, it was so sore; only two round open wounds where the saddle went, as wide across as my two hands, raw and running with pus, which streamed from the edges of his blanket down to his hams. But one had to ride him all the same, jogging on and on. . . . [28]

In Céline's novels you find the victim that Sade never faced (outside of *Justine*); and you find a compassion for him that never sounds false. In fact, Céline raises this compassion to the level of a principle that guides his writing:

The greatest defeat, in anything, is to forget, and above all to forget what it is that smashed you, and to let yourself be smashed without ever realizing how thoroughly devilish men can be. When our time is up, we people mustn't bear malice, but neither must we forget: we must tell the whole thing, without altering one word—everything that we have seen of man's viciousness; and then it will be over and time to go. That is enough of a job for a whole lifetime.[29]

Of course this is the opposite of Sade's whole approach; Céline here is putting himself in the place of the victim. He is not, like Hogarth, simply threatening, or recommending retaliation, but he is giving a tongue and a will to the victim that express a deeper resistance to cruelty than any of which we have spoken thus far. If you are looking for a more particularized contrast between Sade's view of victimization and others', you would do well to think of the Céline who wrote *Journey to the End of the Night*.

In conclusion, let us go back to the idea of example in Hogarth and Sade. As in all other matters, Hogarth is straightforward: example for him was a means to reform, a way of influencing the actions of the audience, through influencing their passion *in terorem,* as he put it in his limping Latin. Hogarth was exhorting us to action like a true Pragmatist.

But Sade, like an Existentialist, was exhorting us to passion. He was not simply telling us what to do. As we have seen, he was an imagination speaking to other imaginations, an individual, cajoling, reassuring, scandalizing, inflaming other individuals into imagining the way he imagined, with his attitude toward cruelty.

That is, Sade was not *simply* out to change men's actions. His task was much broader. As he put it in "The Idea of the Novel" (*Idée sur les Romans*):

> ... it is the heart of man, that most singular of products, and not at all virtue [that the novel must express]; however beautiful, however necessary virtue may be ... [virtue] is still only one of the aspects of this astonishing heart ... the novel, faithful mirror of the heart, must necessarily paint all the folds of man's amazing heart.[30]

His two "didactic" novels, *Justine* and *Juliette,* for example, end with the triumph of vice in one case and with the defeat of virtue in the other, but this does not mean that Sade is simply encouraging vice and discouraging virtue. It means that such results are more interesting novelistically or even humanly speaking than the sentimentalism of virtue triumphant. They alone engage our passionate imagining. As he puts it in *Idée:*

> ... when virtue triumphs, when things are what they should be, our tears are dried before they can flow; but if after harsh trials, we see in the end virtue crushed by vice, our souls necessarily [*indispensablement*] are torn apart, and the work having moved us greatly ... unerringly produces interest, which alone insures praise.[31]

He was closer to being an esthetic purist, a precursor of art for art's sake, than was Hogarth, who wanted to help change society through his "pictur'd morals."

But in this same brief essay, which seems to be a straightforward statement of his intentions, he states his view of nature, and thereby implies, since nature for him was identical with the real and the desirable, that his libertines were examples of what he wanted vigorous beings to *be* and to *do:*

... nature, more bizarre than moralists paint it ... uniform in its plans, irregular in its effects, its bosom always agitated like the living center of a volcano which throws out sometimes precious stones for the service of man, sometimes balls of fire to destroy him; nature, great when she peoples the earth with Antonines and Titus, frightful when she vomits forth an Andronicus or Nero; but always sublime, always majestic ... we must imitate with our sentiments her grandeur, her energy, whatever may be the results.[32]

Of course he is talking about the writing of novels, and about the "heart of man," not about overt actions in the world. But actions and passions are not separate. The echoes from his frequent exhortations to "follow your most monstrous drives no matter what the consequences" are clear. After all of Sade's subtleties and evasions, it is plain that an exhortation to do just this is a part of Sade's whole intent as a writer: he wanted not only to interest his reader, not only to inflame his imagination, but to instruct him in how to think and act in the world.

Still, his overarching idea is: Be cruel. Boil now. Live, *now*, you strong ones.

HORROR AND THE PARADOX

OF CRUELTY

Our topic is personal, individual cruelty—the maiming unto death of one person by another person. We are not yet discussing institutional cruelty, where the victimizer is a whole nation (like England or Holland or America victimizing her colonies), or a compact majority (like the white people of America victimizing the Indians and the Negroes). As we shall see in the next chapter, institutional cruelty is usually too efficient to be exciting to study—it usually grinds its victims not in those dramatic incidents we read about in most histories, but with the sanction of day-to-day customs and a large apparatus of catch-words and justifications. It grinds them slowly, smoothly, and exceeding small. And the grinder, the victimizer, is usually a faceless establishment, not a single person into whose eyes we can stare with a personal curiosity.

But our topic is even narrower than personal cruelty. Personal cruelty can be as smoothly justifiable by catch-words and rationalizations as public cruelty usually is. As we have seen, it can be *quiet*, smooth. Consider again the first plate of Hogarth's *Marriage à la Mode*: the two fathers are making a business deal; they are buying and selling their respective children. The bourgeois father is buying a title for his daughter by marrying her to a young nobleman for money, and the older nobleman is getting money for giving that title and his son to the daughter.

63

They are being chained together—just as the dogs in the fore-ground are chained to each other—quietly, for respectable reasons (their fathers need money or prestige, and besides "Father knows best"). Quiet, personal cruelty is a good friend, even a close relative, of public, institutional cruelty—it destroys its victims smoothly, using customs, catch-words, and justifications to grease the gears of the mill-wheels.

Our topic here is violent, dramatic cruelty that involves screams, often bloodshed, and no smoothly efficient customs, catch-words or rationalizations. *Personal violence*, the kind of violence Sade's whole philosophy exhibits and defends, is especially fascinating (an important word) because both the victimizer and the victim have faces, personalities with which we can empathize or which we can hate or fear, or at least which can be objects of our curiosity.

Now we shall consider personal violence as it appears in the form of the most sensationalistic kind of literature—the horror tale. This often meretricious type of literature flourished in various times and countries and can be broken down into various sub-types.[1] It produced many of its masterpieces in Britain between Christmas of 1764 (when Sir Horace Walpole published *The Castle of Otranto*) and 1820 (when the Irish Anglican minister named C.R. Maturin published *Melmoth the Wanderer*). For the sake of clarity we shall emphasize those works (usually called "Gothic Tales").

The world of the Gothic or terror tale is a hierarchy of power. God is at the top; the Devil is one step down; ecclesiastical and secular aristocracy is another step down; usually silly, chattering servants are one step beneath them; and at the bottom there is usually a helpless maiden or an unarmed youth—the victim. This hierarchy is not as neat and clear as the word "hierarchy" suggests: it involves vast, indefinite powers, saturated by darkness, brooding over and trying to destroy the powerless victim at the bottom of the hierarchy. The experience of that indefinite threat and the definite destruction that follows it is what is called "horror." Horror (at least in the horror tale) is an experience of cruelty being exerted fascinatingly and violently by a single personal force upon a single personal victim.

Sade did not produce horror tales partly because he—like

Hogarth—was an Enlightenment thinker through and through. The powers he celebrated were definite, carefully delineated—the villain was big, passionate, and protected from punishment by such-and-such arrangements; his power, though large, had to be shored up by particular personal and physical conditions. The power of the Devil, or of his deputy Melmoth, in *Melmoth the Wanderer*, is all around his victims, like night air. The power of God, or of Saint Nicholas, is *there*, all around Manfred the Prince of Otranto in *The Castle of Otranto*. Our chapters on cruelty have formed a progression from less to more powerful victimizers, and the same progression occurs within Hogarth's *Cruelty* engravings, as Nero moves from maiming smaller animals to destroying a person. Now we are in the presence of ultimate personal power, the kind of power one approaches with awe and horror, not with simple, localized fear. What we shall be doing is seeing how the victim endures, or is crushed by, this kind of power. Having seen this, we can go on in our last chapter to the world not of novels and engravings but of actual cruelty perpetrated by the institutional equivalent of the victimizer in the Gothic Tale, the Majority.

Power in men and in divinities or devils is like power in the physical world: it is the capacity to overcome resistance and to do it relatively swiftly. This resistance can be mental or physical or both. In horror tales—especially the classic English and American ones—the victims, who are at the bottom of the hierarchy, resist the power of those above them in the hierarchy. And in order to get the happy ending of these romantic novels, the victim is, amazingly enough, successful. We shall be considering this vital point later; but the point here is that the victim exerts resistance (unlike Sade's victims). In studying how all this happens in such sensationalistic and picturesque works as horror tales we can see the dynamics of cruelty—*and the dynamics of its cure*—writ large.

The power of the Gothic villain is vast enough to require theological tools for its analysis; his power is so indefinite and immense—at least at the beginning—and the medieval hierarchy with God and the Devil at the top is so important that the language of theology seems called for. Let us employ it to lay bare the horror of the horror tale.

In his remarkable book *The Idea of the Holy* Rudolph Otto offers us some useful terms for such an analysis. The experience of the holy, what Otto calls the "Numinous" experience, has three aspects. It is an encounter with something mysterious (*mysterium*); it is an encounter with something tremendous (*tremendum*); and it is an encounter that is fascinating (*fascinosum*).[2]

By the *mysterium* Otto means that which is beyond our common sense or scientific understanding, beyond the familiar, beyond the lucid conceptions and perceptions that are so useful in science and everyday life. It has little to do with the "mystery" of a "murder mystery," which eventually makes all things clear in terms of common sense and science. The Numinous experience has to do with things forever hidden, esoteric, extraordinary—in short with forces "wholly other" than the reasonable and the quotidian.

The Gothic Tale trades in the extraordinary. Written in eighteenth- or nineteenth-century England, it is usually set in the Spain or Italy of the Middle Ages. Written during the rationalistic, pragmatic Enlightenment, its medieval castles are surrounded by terrifying storms and inhabited by magic and miracles. Consider the main protagonist of the most ambitious of all the Gothic Tales, *Melmoth the Wanderer*. For one hundred and fifty years Melmoth has wandered around the earth, transporting himself magically where and when he wished, looking for someone to take his place in Hell. He seeks someone so eager to get away from worldly tortures that he will sell his soul to the Devil in order to rid himself of his earthly miseries. And so Melmoth drives men to despair, to hunger, to frustrated love, to all the horrors he can devise, and then asks his victims the question: will you take my place in Hell for all eternity if I rescue you from Hell on earth here and now?

To the mind of a man of the Enlightenment, and to our minds, these are indeed "wholly other" persons and events. They are not puzzles beyond our reasoning powers; they are not *just* beyond our fingertips. They are—or they are intended to be— wholly other than our normal reasoning powers, as different from everyday or scientific life as infinity is from finite things.

But if radical strangeness is important to the Numinous experience, so is the notion of the *tremendum*. Immense energy, overpowering in its capacity to remove obstacles, restless, limitless, forever active, this daunting energy has little or nothing to do with some people's idea of divinity as an intimate, affectionate confidant. In describing religious experience this way, Otto emphasizes the God of the Old Testament who created man and dominates his history with vast and unfailing energy.

In the Gothic Tale this immense energy is communicated in many ways. It appears in the villain in the form of eyes "which no human glance could meet unappalled" in the case of Melmoth, or in the form of "eyes . . . with all their blaze of basilisk horror" in the case of Count Dracula in Bram Stoker's modern novel. In all the Gothic Tales, early and late, the eyes of the villain express power coiled and ready to strike, what Mrs. Radcliffe in *The Mysteries of Udolpho* calls "the strong and terrible energies of the soul."[3] They express powerful passions, unswerving resolution and concentration, and they imply a physical strength as great as the mental, as "daunting," to use Otto's word. Down to his core, the Gothic villain or the Devil he embodies, is restless, ever-active energy, energy always intensified by single-mindedness. Every villain has a master passion—Manfred in *Otranto* needs the body of Isabella; Melmoth needs a soul; M.G. Lewis's Monk needs sex; Dracula needs blood; James' ghosts need the souls of those children. This single-mindedness makes their otherwise immense energies even more immense, just as a lion stalking a zebra is more daunting than a well-fed lion lying in the grass. The only power greater than these powers is the power of God—a power always coiled to strike, at least in the Gothic Tale.

But to look into the eyes of the villains is not to see the full force of the *tremendum* of the Gothic Tale. That force is embodied in the *ambiente*, the time and place in which those villains prey on their victims. The place is often a castle whose lord is the villain. And the castle, as Maturin puts it towards the beginning of *Melmoth*, is

> . . . fortified from top to bottom—not a loophole for pleasure to get in by,—the loopholes were only for arrows; all denoted military power and despotic subjugation à *l'outrance*. . . .[4]

A medieval castle was a fortress with one purpose: to maintain and intensify the power of its lord. Medieval castles came into being when nobles were comparatively independent of their kings, and could with impunity exert absolute power upon anyone living in or near them. It is just such impregnable power that the castle expresses in the Gothic Tale.

And one reason it expresses this power has to do with the victims or prisoners of its lord. When they are in the dungeon of a lord's castle, their weakness is as total as his power. The castle heightens the power of the villain and the weakness of his victim by making it impossible for the victim to escape the "danger" or dominion of the lord, and equally impossible for him to get help from the outside, since even if his cries could be heard through all that distance and stone, his allies would have to "storm" an impregnable fortress

We shall come back to that word "storm" presently, but meanwhile we should notice that throughout this study, in Hogarth's engravings, and in Sade's novels, cruelty occurs most readily in sequestered areas in which the dominion of the powerful one is inescapable and impregnable, at least for the moment. Whether it be a dungeon in a medieval castle or a group of boys gathered round to see a bird have its eyes burned out in a London street, sequestration from escape and resistance is important to cruelty. By heightening the strength of the strong one and by rendering the victim more passive, the castle helps generate and maintain the difference of power that helps make cruelty, like a spark of electricity, possible. The castle is the dynamo of cruelty.

But not only the castle contributes to the impression of an immensity of energy in the villain. Conditions of light and of weather are also part of his *ambiente*. In *Melmoth*, the finest essay on Gothic horror, as well as the most mature Gothic novel, Maturin describes a Moorish fortress as the expression of man's "rage of power," and he goes on to describe it as a

> . . . solid and heavy mass . . . no light playing between its imper-
> meable walls—the image of power, dark, isolated, impenetrable.[5]

The darkness (what M.G. Lewis calls the "gothic obscurity") of a castle dungeon expresses the isolation and helplessness of the victim within it; no one can see him to help him; he does not know where to turn, because he cannot see; but the lord's power is everywhere: *he* knows his way around the castle, and he can move at will to fall on his prey. The dark places of the earth are the scenes of cruelty because darkness helps isolate the victim from help and helps insulate the victimizer from hindrance.

And there are other elements of the *ambiente* that express and enhance the powers of the victimizer. Storms, for instance. Again we must turn to Maturin for the most effective descriptions. Throughout *Melmoth* he makes winds, clouds, thunder, and lightning allies of the cruel Melmoth, and a tremendous, daunting force for his victims. For Melmoth, thunder is "a kind of wild and terrible energy [that] nerved his frame." For Maturin weather is "an involuntary interpreter between us and our feelings," a way of expressing vast and terrible energies in the world, as well as a way of actually exerting those energies upon the objects of the world. Lightning can come from anywhere, but we, its victims, do not know where or when it will strike as we stand under the wide, black sky. The power of lightning is indefinite, vast, destructive, and so Maturin makes it resemble "the eye of a fiend"[6] both because it is a symptom of immense destructive energies and because it is an immediate threat that those energies will smash you, the passive ones.

Edmund Burke in his essay on the sublime and the beautiful ascribed indefiniteness, vastness to sublimity—a storm is sublime, tremendous with energy and mortality, and in the Gothic Tale it is an indefinite menace to the weak while it is a new source of strength to the strong. A storm polarizes the victimizer and his victim, sharpens the disparity between their powers to overcome resistance, and it makes horror more vivid.

There is a storm early in *Melmoth*,[7] in which a ship is smashed upon the rocks, and the coastal inhabitants watch with dread while the sailors perish almost within reach. But the horror of the scene is not at its peak until the reader is shown the Wanderer standing alone on a crag

> . . . unmoved by the storm, as by the spectacle . . . not a thread of the stranger's garments seemed ruffled by the blast. . . .

And then from the Wanderer come the words "Let them perish," as he stands looking down upon those writhing, dying, screaming men in the sea.

And Maturin goes on to describe how a vast wave smashed the foundering ship and

> ... extorted a cry of horror from the spectators; they felt as if they were echoing that of the victims ...

Then, after that cry the Wanderer sends forth a "laugh that chilled [the] ... blood." The horror of the scene is complete: the Wanderer and the storm have worked together in the destruction of feeble human life. The difference between the power of the victimizer and the weakness of the victim is at its most striking. The Gothic Tale uses storms, castles, and demonic men to increase that difference and thus to heighten the cruelty being perpetrated.

There is one more moment in Otto's discussion of Numinous experience that is of importance to us, not only for understanding the horror in the Gothic Tale, but for understanding cruelty in general. The tremendous, incomprehensible force of the "Numen" or the divine has the quality of *fascinosum:* it entrances us, fascinates us. We feel an impulse to make those energies part of *ourselves*, its victims. In the midst of our terror there is an impulse for self-surrender, a yearning that believers call "love." This yearning does not light up the darkness; here love is, indeed, blind; this yearning is full of terror and the darkness of the understanding. It is the *Noche oscura* of Saint John of the Cross.

Not all Gothic Tales explore relentlessly and subtly this ambivalence of the victim towards her victimizer. In *The Castle of Otranto* there is no such subtlety. But in *The Monk* Antonia, the victim, feels at her first encounter with Ambrosio the Monk

> ... a pleasure fluttering in her bosom which till then had been unknown to her ... when at length the friar spoke, the sound of his voice seemed to penetrate into her very soul ... no other of the spectators felt such violent sensations as did the young Antonia. ... [8]

The victim feels love in the presence of such energies, and such danger. The victimizer draws and holds the attention, the admiration, the awe of his victim, just as a cat sometimes holds the attention of the bird it is stalking.

This fascination occurs throughout *Melmoth*, in various forms. The most sustained relationship the Wanderer has with any of his victims is his relationship with Isidora (whom he has "married" with the help of a dead priest, revived for the occasion). She is deeply in love with him, even while she is in terror of him. And in all instances when Melmoth is ready to seize a victim and inflict the dreadful choice of destruction now or destruction *then*, in all such instances, the victim hears

> . . . a strain of music, soft, solemn, and delicious, breathed round him, audibly ascending from the ground, and increasing in sweetness and power. . . . [9]

As usual, Maturin, as fine a psychological analyst as he is ingenious as a novelist, finds an exact expression for this fascination. The young monk Monçada is being tortured for trying to leave the monastery, and the persecution he has suffered has all but killed him. Now he is going through still another trial by his inhuman, villainous superiors; he finds himself

> . . . deprecating their *worst*, but defying, almost desiring it, in the terrible and indefinite curiosity of despair. . . . [10]

This terrible and indefinite curiosity of despair is nowhere more strikingly seen than in the type of horror tale that came into popularity after the Golden Age of the Gothic, the vampire tale as an art form. These tales are not as ambitious as the novels of Maturin or of Mrs. Radcliffe, but they in some ways distill the sensation of horror in the victim. Sheridan Le Fanu's *Carmilla* describes the victim's attitude towards the vampire:

> . . . I experienced a strange tumultuous excitement that was pleasurable, ever and anon, mingled with a vague sense of fear and disgust. . . . I was conscious of a love growing into adoration, and also of abhorrence. This I know is a paradox, but I can make no further attempt to explain the feeling.[11]

One of the most striking instances in literature of this paradoxical feeling is the scene in another vampire tale, *Dracula*, wherein one of Dracula's victims, Jonathan Harker, is lying on a bed in Dracula's castle while Dracula's three vampire sisters are bending over him getting ready to drink his blood; one sister speaks:

> "He is young and strong; there are kisses for us all." I lay quiet, looking out under my eyelashes in an agony of delightful anticipation. The fair girl advanced and bent over me till I could feel the movement of her breath upon me. Sweet it was in one sense, honey-sweet, and sent the same tingling through the nerves as her voice, but with a bitter underlying the sweet, a bitter offensiveness, as one smells in blood.
>
> I was afraid to raise my eyelids, but looked out and saw perfectly under the lashes. The girl went on her knees, and bent over me, simply gloating. There was a deliberate voluptuousness which was both thrilling and repulsive, and as she arched her neck she actually licked her lips like an animal. . . . Lower and lower went her head as the lips went below the range of my mouth and chin and seemed about to fasten on my throat. Then she paused, and I could hear the churning sound of her tongue as it licked her teeth and lips, and could feel the hot breath on my neck. . . . I closed my eyes in a languorous ecstasy and waited—waited with beating heart.[12]

Dracula cannot enter a house without being invited in; Melmoth's greatest cruelties are preceded by sweet music. What Conrad calls "fascination with the abomination" is an important element in the most careful articulations authors have made of victimization in the horror tale. It is true that the "ambiguous feeling" frequently has sexual drives at its center: Dracula, for example, gets blood only by "kissing" (in her bedroom) a beautiful young victim, and it is his sisters who perpetrate the horror on Harker.

This is no place to explore all forms of the *fascinosum*, including erotic mysticism (as in Saint John of the Cross and others). The "terrible and indefinite curiosity of despair," the felt paradox of adoration and abhorrence that Le Fanu describes can take various forms; but in the Gothic Tale, and, as we shall see, in history, it aways helps strengthen the iron bonds that tie the victim to her victimizer, that keep her in his "danger."

And this "curiosity" is important to the spectator's or reader's relationship with the cruelties of the Gothic Tale. He too feels this awe before immense power, he too "identifies" with both the suffering victim and the acting villain. Like the horror of the victim, his horror is a commingling of desire and disgust, of admiration and the desire to participate in immense power, as well as fear for his own life. Again we can turn to Maturin for the striking insight. He calls all those with a curiosity for human suffering *"amateurs in suffering."* He goes on:

> ... that excitement which the sight of suffering never fails to give, from the spectacles of a tragedy, or an *auto-da-fé*, down to the writhings of the meanest reptile on whom you can inflict torture, and feel that torture is the result of your own power ... is a species of feeling of which we never can divest ourselves ... suffering is always an indication of weakness,—we glory in our impenetrability ... [13]

In the actual victim, according to various Gothic Tales, this glorying in impenetrability takes the form of admiration, even love of the cruel one while he is coiled to strike. And in the spectator there is a sense of identity or empathy with both the sufferer and the agent of that suffering. This double identity is the "terrible and indefinite curiosity of despair" we call "horror."

The curiosity that draws us to witness and even to suffer cruelty is one of the reasons why cruelty towards human beings (as well as towards other animals) has persisted; absent-minded, quiet cruelty has other motives, like the motives of those fathers in the first plate of Hogarth's *Marriage;* but the fact that cruelty can be both detestable and delectable at the same time helps explain not only the persistence of cruelty in history, but the esthetic appeal of cruelty in literature and the arts. This fact when put into words becomes a paradox. "Pleasure in pain" has fascinated—as a paradoxical phrase *and* as an experience—not only Sade himself but others more conscious of their craft as writers. What Mario Praz in his *The Romantic Agony* calls the "mysterious bond between pleasure and suffering"[14] appears in Percy Bysshe Shelley's poem on the Medusa:

> . . .
> Its horror and its beauty are divine.
> Upon its lips and eyelids seems to lie
> Loveliness like a shadow, from which shine,

Fiery and lurid, struggling underneath,
The agonies of anguish and of death.
Yet it is less the horror than the grace
    Which turns the gazer's spirit into stone
. . .
    'Tis the melodious hue of beauty thrown
Athwart the darkness and the glare of pain,
Which humanize and harmonize the strain.[15]

And Praz gives other instances of the estheticizing of cruelty. Joseph Conrad in his brief masterpiece *Heart of Darkness*, expressed his fascination (with both the fact and its paradoxical expressions) in various ways, including "the strange commingling of desire and hate,"[16] which in itself is a useful definition of "horror."

And the affective fact—usually unverbalized, and therefore quite unparadoxical to us—occurs in the mild pleasures we find in bloodless victories (a prize won that others failed to win, a promotion received that others failed to get) as well as in our snarls of pleasure at an especially fierce boxing match, or in our delicious tears falling at a sad but satisfying play, poem, or novel. Gustave Flaubert wrote of man's "dark depths that must be appeased" (*fond noir à contenter*)[17] by this combination of delight and disgust, and modern depth psychologists have analyzed it in terms of the "Id" or similar forces in man.

Those dark depths were being appeased when that Father of the Church Tertullian tried to keep Christians from going to cruel public spectacles by urging them to remember that they, as Christians, have their own spectacles. As Christians they will see these spectacles in heaven, where there will be

> . . . the charioteer to watch, red all over in the wheel of flame; and, next, the athletes to be gazed upon, not in their gymnasiums but hurled in the fire. . . . Such sights, such exaltation—what praetor, consul, quaestor, priest will ever give you of his bounty? . . . [18]

And he adds, reminding us of Sade's pleas for the imaginative life:

> And yet all these, in some sort, are ours, pictured through faith in the imagination of the spirit. . . . Things of greater joy than circus, theater, or amphitheater. . . . [19]

Indeed, Hogarth himself, for all his humane intentions, had to give examples of cruelty in his "pictur'd morals," not of well-being. He tried to do a series on a happy family, but gave it up. In order to "delight and instruct" he had to give examples of human beings destroying each other.

In the arts and in life there is man's *fond noir à contenter*, and the appeasing of those depths, whether by fictive or real cruelties, is what is meant by "horror." The Gothic Tale is only one instance of the appeasement which satisfies man's "terrible and indefinite curiosity."

In fairness to Otto's careful analysis of the religious experience, it must be noticed that *his* use of the *mysterium tremendum et fascinosum* has to do with the Numinous experience man has of God, an experience that transcends good and evil, and any other human categories. Except for the top of the Gothic Tale's hierarchy of power, where God resides, Otto's use of these terms does not apply precisely to the Gothic Tale, where villains are, not simply "tremendous and fascinating mysteries," but *evil*.

In Eckermann's *Conversations with Goethe* we find the Numinous experience cut down to a villain's size in Goethe's description of the "daemonic." There he points out that the daemonic is beyond our comprehension, ferociously energetic, and fascinating. The daemonic creature does not appear in "a clear, prosaic city like Berlin,"[20] but lives in the dark, strange places of the world. As Goethe puts it in *Poetry and Truth:*

> This daemonic character appears in its most *dreadful* form when it stands out dominatingly in some man . . . such men seldom have any goodness of heart to recommend them. But an incredible force goes forth from them and they exercise an incredible power over all creatures, nay perhaps even over the elements. And who can say how far such an influence may not extend? . . . [21]

In *Conversations* Goethe says that Mephistopheles is "much too negative a being" to be called "daemonic,"[22] and he might have said the same about the Gothic villain. But both terms—the

"Numinous" and the "daemonic"—share the emphasis on incomprehensible, immense, restless, and fascinating energy at work upon the minds and bodies of the weak. The fact remains that God and Gothic villains must be kept distinct in our minds or we misread Otto, the Bible, and the Gothic Tales.

There is another reason why it can be misleading to be satisfied with terms like "Numinous" and even "daemonic" in understanding cruelty and horror in the Gothic Tale. For Goethe and for Otto the weak ones do not resist successfully. They are "enthralled" (a word we have used before): they are both psychologically and physically enslaved, made the thralls of God or the daemonic creature.

Not so in the Gothic Tale. The victim is fascinated, and she is weak, but no well-developed character suffering the force of the divine or the daemonic ever *breaks*, ever surrenders with the total surrender of absolute faith or the total surrender of the hypnotized bird. In all the classic Gothic Tales the resistance of the victim is so great that the villain is always the loser.

Consider Melmoth. He is a daemonic version of Mozart's Don Giovanni (or perhaps the Don himself is also daemonic): both of them are glorious, but they are constantly running into stone walls, into frustration. Even Isidora refuses Melmoth's proposal, though she loves him, and so do the other victims he stalks. In *The Monk* Antonia, innocent and weak as she is, resists Ambrosio to the end. Isabella refuses Manfred unhesitatingly in *Otranto*, and her allies defeat him in the end. And in our own time, Henry James' exquisite version of the Gothic Tale, *The Turn of the Screw*, ends with the little boy fighting Peter Quint's ghost until "his little heart, dispossessed, had stopped."[23]

There are exceptions in the history of the Gothic Tale, cases where resistance to the villain is not an issue, is not even conceivable. For instance, shortly after Count Dracula interrupts his sisters as they were beginning their blood feast in the castle, Dracula placates them by pointing to a bag he was carrying

> . . . which he had thrown upon the floor, and which moved as though there were some living thing within it. . . . One of the women jumped forward and opened it. If my ears did not deceive me there was a gasp and a low wail, as of a half-smothered child. . . .[24]

And others die without resistance—but they are as incapable of resistance as that infant.

Usually it is not a case of refusal *or* acceptance, resistance *or* compliance—usually it is *both* that operate at the same time, as we have seen. Melmoth's victims not only hear the "exquisite sounds" that precede the temptation, but they find it almost impossible "to escape the horrible fascination of that unearthly glare" in his eyes. As we have noticed, they feel curiosity, a kind of suspenseful waiting for the powerful one to pounce on them, a "delicious agony."[25]

But the victim is not the only one who feels this ambivalence. Melmoth has his moments of compassion and even love; Manfred in *Otranto* feels great remorse, and Ambrosio the Monk, after he has raped Antonia, "felt himself at once repulsed from and attracted towards her . . . . There was something in her look which penetrated him with horror . . . conscience pointed out to him the whole extent of his crime . . . ."[26] And so the "ambiguous feeling" of horror is felt by the victim, the audience, and the villain.

None of these resistances—within the villain or from the victim—is to be found in Sade's stories and dialogues. The victim simply crumples, and even Justine feels no anger or disgust but only pain. In the Gothic Tale almost every victim fights, and often the villains fight within their own souls—power, indefinite and great as it may be, is ambiguous.

In fact, in the end, so powerfully does the victim usually fight back—either alone or with her allies—that the ending of the horror tale is almost always (short modern stories excepted) the story of the destruction of the villain. The Gothic Tale, utterly unlike Sade, has a very simple conventional morality behind it: its authors despise torture and killing. Maturin, for example, talks with disgust about those who " . . . devour animals, and torture from abused vegetables a drink, that, without quenching thirst, has the power of extinguishing reason, inflaming passion, and shortening life. . . . "[27] Innocence, kindness, reciprocity of service, these are the positive morality of all the horror tales.

But with this reciprocity of action goes a belief in the reciprocity of victimization. All the vast powers of the victimizer are matched, usually at the ending, by the vast powers of the victim's allies, and are turned against him. Most Gothic Tales have a "happy ending" suitable for their subject matter—horror. Melmoth dies in such pain and spiritual travail that no eyes can tolerate it or words describe it. Manfred's sins in *Otranto* are not as terrifying as his castle itself, and so he is not punished severely. But Ambrosio, the Monk! He is mentally and physically tortured to the extreme of human endurance; he signs his contract with the Devil moments before he learns of his release from punishment (and he signs it to avoid the horrors of prison and torture); but his contract fails to give him life, power or pleasure—it gives him only death. And besides suffering he feels remorse, chagrin for his own stupidity in signing so soon—here are some sentences from the last paragraph of *The Monk:*

> . . . darting his talons into the monk's shaven crown, the [Devil] sprang with him from the rock. The caves and mountains rang with Ambrosio's shrieks. The daemon continued to soar aloft, till reaching a dreadful height, he released the sufferer. Headlong fell the monk through the airy waste; the sharp point of a rock received him; and he rolled from precipice to precipice, till, bruised and mangled, he rested on the river's banks. . . . The sun now rose above the horizon; its scorching beams darted full upon the head of the expiring sinner. Myriads of insects were called forth by the warmth; they drank the blood which trickled from Ambrosio's wounds; he had no power to drive them from him. . . . The eagles of the rock tore his flesh piecemeal, and dug out his eye-balls with their crooked beaks . . . six miserable days did the villain languish. On the seventh a violent storm arose: the winds in fury rent up rocks and forests: the sky was now black with clouds, now sheeted with fire: the rain fell in torrents: it swelled the stream; the waves overflowed their banks; they reached the spot where Ambrosio lay, and when they abated, carried with them into the river the corse of the despairing monk.[28]

And this is the happy ending of a horror tale.

Whenever I read this, especially the passage about the talons in the monk's shaven crown, I remember the last of Hogarth's *Cruelty* engravings. The same reciprocity of harm-doing obtains—down to the penetration of the shaven skull; and there is the same pleasure-disgust in witnessing destruction. The grievances of the weak under the hitherto vast and indefinite power of the strong have to be redressed—a debt must be payed to the weak and their sympathizers. The payment tortures and destroys the victimizer *at least* as penetratingly as he tortured and destroyed his victims. He, too, becomes a powerless victim ("he had no power to drive them from him") under forces as superior to his as his forces were superior to his victim's. He, too, suffers maiming and destruction, just as his victims did. He thus pays his debt to the universe; the scales are balanced.

The curious point of all this is that the terminal horrors of the Gothic Tale—the writhings and screamings of a Dracula transfixed by a bowie knife in his heart while his head is being cut off by a great Kukri knife—is a happy ending for an audience that presumably believes in a conventional morality of kindness and reciprocity of help. The horrors of the ending of a horror tale are as ambiguous as the horrors that make it up. The same morality that enjoins us to be kind and to help the weak can enjoin us to be cruel to the erstwhile strong and to destroy them when they are powerless (Dracula could not rise to defend himself at the end of the story—it was not yet night).

Of course the victim's suffering was "undeserved"—she was "innocent"; and the victimizer's suffering was "deserved"—he was "guilty." And so one kind of suffering creates a debt that has to be paid and the other pays that debt. Moreover, punishment can prevent future sufferings. These are issues I leave to students of jurisprudence and morality.

But it is plain that the Gothic Tale with all its horrors shows how the maiming of a life can be an object of both desire and loathing for the victim and for the reader, and this ambiguous feeling is *shared* by Sadists, with their desire for collision with conventional kindness-moralities, and by moralists who believe in conventional moralities.

And it is also plain that in the most spectacular victimizations literature offers, the victim strikes back in various ways. The Gothic Tale shows the various resistances the victim exerts. True, she is fascinated, in awe of the indefinite power of the victimizer; and true, she is weaker and therefore is passive, and so allows the active villain—at first—to work his will upon her. But she can resist to the end, and that resistance is a call to action not only to the other characters in the novel but to the reader as well, a call that unites victims against victimizers in order to upset the hierarchy of power.

The main point of talking about these endings is that the cruelties that happen to the villain are indeed endings, terminal cruelties. Some cruelties are *provocative;* they call for consequences. Other cruelties are *responsive*—they answer that call and end the story. There is a consummation, a consummatory cruelty in the horror tale that is one of its horrors, but different from all the rest. Its sense is a sense of completeness, of repayment, of rounding out. It is, presumably, *a cruelty that will not escalate or be repaid.* A power crushes the villain and the cruelties are over.

We must remember that we are discussing novels, traditional novels, not modern unplotted ones: these novels have beginnings, middles, and ends—and these ends are important to the form, the unity, the completeness of the novels. These novels are not simply one event after another, like the tick-tock of clocks; they do not deal simply with what Frank Kermode in *The Sense of an Ending* calls mere *chronos.* They deal with what he calls *kairos,* a period of time that is a "significant season,"[29] a completion charged with meaning, a completion that gives meaning to all the events that preceded it. In memory now we feel that the meaning of all those horrible victimizations is that they had to be atoned for, that they incurred a debt that had to be paid; and now that the debt has been paid the book is done. The provocative and the responsive cruelties of a horror story together rescue the novel's time from being "humanly uninteresting successiveness," like the ticking of a clock. And they rescue it by laying a terminal cruelty upon the head of the one who has been perpetrating the incitative ones.

In the Gothic Tale we are in a realm of the arts wherein the reader's action in response to the work is minimized. Hogarth wanted to stop the cruelty in the streets, as his autobiographical notes point out. He said there that he was prouder of those *Cruelty* engravings than if he had painted Raphael's "cartoons" at Hampton Court; and he added that, of course, he spoke as a man, not necessarily as an artist. The point is that he could separate the two and state a moral. The didacticism of Sade is not so definite. It is blunted by the fact that Sade saw himself as much a stimulator and student of imaginations as a teacher trying to make us perform particular murderous actions. He wanted to make us boil, at least in our imaginations. In the Gothic Tale moral didacticism is even more diluted: is *Dracula* trying to teach us not to trust Hungarian Counts? Walpole himself in the Preface to *Otranto* laments the weakness of its "moral." Here a desire to produce a satisfying esthetic experience is *inseparable* from any desire to produce a satisfying moral experience (according to the conventional moralities that revolve around the Golden Rule). The moral of a Gothic Tale is usually dubious.

The Gothic Tale sees the particular victim as powerful, just as Hogarth did, but the Gothic novelist's power operates in medieval times and faraway lands, not in the everyday streets of London. And so whatever the Gothic novelist has to teach is more removed from immediate action than were Hogarth's *Cruelty* plates. The same applies to Sade's novels; they are about (Sade's) modern times, are set in *almost* reachable places (like Silling), and are about *almost* recognizable aristocracy—but they are aphrodisiacs and portraits for the imagination at least as much as they are attempts to change our actions in specific ways. The tale of horror is even more removed from quotidian action and from straightforward moral didacticism.

But the curious fact remains that Hogarth and these Romantic-sensationalistic novels glorify the power of the victim, and glorify especially her power to victimize her victimizer. Here, as we have noticed, the moral and the esthetic come together (in a successful Gothic Tale) to produce an esthetic *cum* moral consummation.

In *Melmoth*, Maturin points out that "The drama of terror has the irresistible power of converting its audience into its victims."[30] He claims throughout the book that the witnesses of actual horrors and the readers of horror tales mimic the passions and screams of the victims. Perhaps an ending is successful not from the conviction that a moral debt has been discharged, but from the sense of a removal of the villain from "our" backs.

Whatever the explanation, in the successful Gothic Tale the satisfaction of the victim in the terminal responsive horror is parallel to our satisfaction as readers, and all these horrors *together* make of the successful horror tale not mere history, not simply one damned thing after another, but a *kairos*, a whole that is consummated. And the significance in Kermode's "significant season" is that now, after the ending, there is no more cruelty here. We are purged. The debt is paid. Choose your metaphor and pursue it where you will. The point is that there is peace after the "happy" ending of a horror tale. There is no more cruelty: there are no more victims. We may need horror, but we also need peace. And that peace comes out of an awareness of being *free* from the daunting and fascinating power of the victimizer, and free from the long threat of destruction.

This need for both horror and peace is another form of the paradox we have considered early in this chapter when we were studying Flaubert's *fond noir à contenter* and Conrad's "strange commingling of desire and hate." In general it may be said that **the paradox of cruelty is this : the destruction of men (as well as of animals) is both readily justifiable (in terms of stimulation,** economic or social need, etc.), and totally unjustifiable. Deliberate destruction of a human being is impossible to defend conclusively, and history is full of the deliberate—self-congratulatory—destruction of human beings. When we think about the destruction of a human life, we can, in a certain situation or in a certain mood find many convincing reasons for perpetrating that destruction; but if we start our deliberations in a different situation or in a different mood we can find it utterly impossible to justify that destruction. And, as we have been seeing, *when* we perpetrate that destruction, we can *both* abhor it *and* enjoy it at the same time.

The paradox of cruelty makes hypocrites or at least self-deceivers of the victimizers : they (for instance the white majority in America) can defend life, liberty, and the pursuit of happiness while torturing the weak in their midst. And they can build ingenious devil's bridges between those words and these deeds; when the bridges feel sound to them, they can walk across them to perpetrate the cruel deeds which give them a not-so-secret disgust and pleasure. And the spectators of destruction can deplore it and look joyfully at it in the same act. Lucretius in the first line of Book II of his *On the Nature of Things* gave this affective form of the paradox its classic statement:

> It is sweet, when on the great sea the winds trouble its waters, to behold from land another's deep distress . . . [31]

He was not talking here about human cruelty to human beings, but the bittersweet taste in the mouth of the spectator of destruction makes us all Maturin's "amateurs in suffering."

The paradox appears also in the victim's mind and actions: she dreads her destruction, and is fascinated, both by her destroyer and by the very act of destruction, as a captive Jew can be fascinated by a Nazi SS leader. But what the paradox does to the victim is rather different from what it does to the victimizer: it does not make a self-deceiver or a hypocrite of her—it paralyzes her, renders her even more passive than she was before. It enchants, enthralls her, makes the will of another her law.

And it does much the same to the horrified, rigid spectator of the action. The only thing he can do in this esthetic trance is to exhibit the etymological origins of the word horror: *horrere*, to bristle, to have one's hair stand on end, and one's body tremble and turn rough with gooseflesh.[32] This is all he can *do*.

But when the victim and her allies break the esthetic trance by resisting the villain, she can defeat him, though he and their *ambiente* are terrific. She can *act* against his will with the help of her allies, and, as we have noticed, this action breaks the spell his power casts over us all and ends the Gothic Tale.

And so the paradox of cruelty can help us to understand more than the Gothic Tale—it can help us to understand cruelty and its cure. As long as men feel and think paradoxically, ambivalently, about cruelty, as long as they love and hate human destruction, there will be popular horror tales, and there will also be personal and public, violent and quiet cruelties perpetrated on the weak. But the horror tales (and the paradox) also show us that there is a shaft of light in the Gothic darkness: the victim and her allies can dissolve the paradox, can resist, and can succeed in stopping the cruelty, just as, at the time of this writing, the black people are resisting ancient cruelties in various quarters of American life.

The form—especially the ending—of the Gothic Tale shows us writ large the best way to dissolve the Paradox of Cruelty and to mitigate man's terrible penchant for piously destroying his fellow man. That way is not the way of long-suffering patience; it is not the way of the maiden who waits for the villain to transform himself miraculously into a virtuous friend. Power seldom, if ever, presides over its own subversion. The victim herself, with her allies, must act, must achieve the power to respond effectively, instead of being patient, and instead of being paralyzed with horror. The horror tale shows us that the power of the victim can be—when she breaks the spell—even more effective than the apparently vast power of the villain. The task for the victim and her allies is to find a way to power that will not provoke new responsive cruelties by creating new victims, but will end the long history of cruelties by upsetting the hierarchy of power and forcing human beings to face each other with a little fear and with much respect.

FROM THE NOVEL TO HISTORY

LIKE Hogarth's *Cruelty* engravings, Harriet Beecher Stowe's *Uncle Tom's Cabin* is a didactic horror tale; its obvious, indeed its avowed, intention is to muster examples of destruction in order to teach its audience an important lesson that is easily detached from the text and immediately applicable to human conduct. In her Preface to the 1852 edition, published eleven years before the Emancipation Proclamation, she states:

> The object of these sketches is to awaken sympathy and feeling for the African race, as they exist among us; to show their wrongs and sorrows, under a system so necessarily cruel and unjust as to defeat and do away the good effects of all that can be attempted for them, by their best friends, under it.[1]

Whether or not it is true—or even meaningful—to say that her book helped bring about the American Civil War, the fact remains that her intention in writing the book was to bring about disgust with American slavery and sympathy with its victims, the black people of America.

A novel with such a definite purpose, and one that uses moral horror as its main instrument, may help to move our discussion of victimization from art into the realities of history, across the silence that surrounds every work of Gothic imagination. This particular novel is especially useful for making this transition because it is about the same realities that our next chapter will treat, and because there is a somewhat conventional horror tale embedded in its last chapter.

The scene of this brief horror tale is Simon Legree's plantation, which is ten miles from its nearest neighbor. One reaches it only by a "wild, forsaken road" that runs through waste lands where the wind whispers sadly, and through cypress swamps thick with poisonous moccasin snakes crawling over broken, rotting stumps under "funereal black moss." These swamps surround—like a moat—the dilapidated house of Simon Legree, the planter who has bought Uncle Tom. The swamps, the guns, the ferocious dogs, and the two brutal lieutenants of Legree together form an apparently insuperable barrier to escape. Once the plantation house was opulent; but now under Legree's ungentle and moneymaking hands it is in decay, with shattered window panes and shutters hanging by a hinge.

In that house only one man's will may operate freely; here he is protected from interference and from loss not only by the physical characteristics of the place and by his ferocious guards, but mainly by the laws of early nineteenth century America, which made it impossible for a slave to testify in any court concerning any actions done upon him by a white man. Legree is the only white man in that house; directly under him are Sambo and Quimbo, who compete with each other in perpetrating cruelties on the other slaves in order to win their master's favor. Under this cruel trinity are more slaves, including Cassy, a beautiful quadroon, who had been Legree's mistress and is now his dedicated enemy. Cassy's body is under his physical power, in his "danger," but her mind has turned against him because of his cruelties.

Once when Legree told her to come sit on his knee and "hear to reason," Cassy replied:

> "Simon Legree, take care!" . . . with a sharp flash of her eye, a glance so wild and insane in its light as to be almost appalling. "You're afraid of me, Simon . . . and you've reason to be! But be careful, for I've got the devil in me!"[2]

And so she had—the secular devil of the aroused victim's hatred for her oppressor. She was going insane with this hatred, was "possessed" by it, and this made her dreadful to Legree, who had a "superstitious horror of insane persons." It was this daemonic hatred that made her mentally more powerful than even the ferocious Simon Legree, who owned her under the law. His too was a restlessly energetic" demoniac heart,"[3] but Cassy hated him single-mindedly, with a mastering passion, like a cat's hunger for a bird. He, on the other hand, simply feared her whenever he happened to be near her. And so she had the upper hand; in the brief horror tale towards the end of the book she uses that dominance to terrify the once terrifying Simon Legree.

With Uncle Tom there came down that long road a pretty young black girl, Emmeline, whom Cassy came to love with a mother's love. Emmeline loathed the filth and dreaded the brutality of bullet-headed Legree, and she had a special reason for her feelings: Legree wanted her to take Cassy's place as his sex partner.

To save Emmeline and herself Cassy's preternaturally active brain develops a stratagem. The garret of the house is a vast, dingy, dark place hung with cobwebs and covered with thick dust. Years before, a negro woman displeased Legree, and he confined her to the garret until she died there under mysterious circumstances. After she was buried, stories were passed about oaths, violent blows, "wailing and groans of despair" being heard coming from the apparently empty garret. Legree is a violently superstitious man, and Cassy decides to use this excitability, and the garret, to save Emmeline and herself.

Her plan is to terrify Legree so that he never wants to come up to that garret—and neither do his servants want to set foot in it. She will ostentatiously escape with Emmeline into the swamp, so that Legree and his brutes will rush out to capture them. But she and Emmeline will double back from the swamp and walk in a stream that flows alongside the plantation house—this will throw the dogs off the scent. Then she will return to the garret while the hunters are looking everywhere but in the place she will be—in the house, in Legree's domain. She and Emmeline will live comfortably in the garret for days after Legree will return from the unsuccessful hunt. During that time she will excite the horror of Legree to such an extent that he will be both fascinated by the garret and profoundly in dread of it. After a sufficient time to make Legree almost insane with terror and weariness of terror, she will take Emmeline out of the house one morning after one of Legree's drunken, orgiastic evenings, and she will simply walk away, well supplied with Legree's money, which she will have stolen easily; and they will escape to Canada.

She carries out her plan. To make Legree feel the indefinite, mysterious, threatening power that alone can cow him, she sets the scene in various ways. Before the feigned escape she puts a bottle into a knothole in the garret and even a mild wind makes the bottle give forth a "doleful and lugubrious wailing" while a high wind emits "a perfect shriek." She waits for

> . . . a stormy, windy night, such as raises whole squadrons of nondescript noises in rickety old houses. Windows were rattling, shutters flapping . . . [4]

Then she puts near Legree's chair a book containing stories of bloody murders and ghostly visitation, all of which have a "strange fascination for one who once begins to read them."[5] She excites Legree's fears of strange, vast powers by hints and rhetorical questions, by fixing her "glittering eyes" upon him while he is coming under her spell; and suddenly, at the height of his dread, she lays a cold hand on his, so that he leaps up with an oath. She counts into the ears of Legree the strokes of the clock at the midnight hour, while he sits stunned under the "keen, sneering glitter" of her black eyes. And in time she escapes with the virginal Emmeline from the plantation, and from America, toward the North Star into freedom.

We misread both this brief tale and the whole book if we think that she has escaped from simply the will of an individual named Simon Legree. True, she and Emmeline have escaped from his lust for destruction, sex, and money; but for Harriet Beecher Stowe they have escaped from slavery, that "system so necessarily cruel." The essence of the system for Harriet Beecher Stowe is the master-slave relationship itself, whatever the accidents of character, time, and place might be.[6] And the relationship is this: an owner has absolute freedom to do what he wills to his absolutely enslaved chattel; and the slave can do nothing that the master disapproves. The master is totally active—the only member of the relationship who can use his initiative broadly; the slave is totally passive—the member of the relationship who has no initiative that can withstand the will of the master. The master is unrestrictedly powerful; the slave is unrestrictedly weak;

the master must not be resisted; the slave cannot resist—he is a zero, as far as his own will is concerned. And men who need money as well as all those other goods that can come if one has actual power over other human beings will get whatever they need—especially if there is nothing to resist their wills. They will easily placate what conscience they may have by rationalizations or forgetting, or they will feel no commands of conscience while they exert their power on another human being and observe the fascinating effects of that power. The slave relationship is unselving a human being, thingifying a living human being, with total immunity.

Cassy and Harriet Beecher Stowe are sisters in the art of creating fictions: they both made fictions for a purpose other than entertainment. And they both believed that the victim can escape destruction not by reasoning patiently with her victimizer, nor even by patient suffering (Uncle Tom, the exemplar of such suffering, is killed slowly and horribly by Legree, though he wins a kind of victory by becoming at the end "disenthralled" from Legree's tortures). Cassy and Harriet Beecher Stowe believe that the victim can escape the destruction of her humanity by victimizing her erstwhile victimizer.

When she is in a position like Cassy's she must find the susceptibilities, the chinks in the armor, of the otherwise all-powerful one, and she must use all of her powers to take advantage of them, to take the initiative at last, to take action. The indefinite, restless, boundless power of a Legree or anyone else living in the "peculiar institution" of slavery had to be matched with the indefinite, restless powers of his erstwhile victims. They certainly could not be matched by neat, cogent reasoning while sitting on Legree's knee and acceding to his request to hear *his* reasons. As Sade saw so well, resistance, obstacles are more effective against immense power than gentle persuasion. Action, evasive as well as frontal, is the water one pours upon the victimizer's fire.

Again it is important to see that Harriet Beecher Stowe was not attacking individuals like Simon Legree, or like slave-owners as a group of individuals. Much of her book is about a gentle, magnanimous slave-owner, Augustine St. Clare, the father of the angelic Eva. She was attacking a system that was itself cruel because its center was the heart of cruelty: total activity smashing total passivity. The system that creates and maintains this relationship is "so necessarily cruel" not because of accidental pains peculiar to particular situations. Pain, as was suggested in the Introduction, is only a symptom, is not in itself the only reason for the doctor's efforts to cure. Nor is it what the doctor spends all his time considering. The disease that pain sometimes symptomizes was what Harriet Beecher Stowe and Cassy were trying to remove; it was the disease of being unselved, utterly passive. And they cured it by turning all their attention to finding freedom from the system that made this disease the law of the land.

We have now left the dream-dungeons of Sade and the medieval castles of the Gothic Tale with all their unbelieved-in miracles and catastrophes; we have left a world where the audience contributes only—or mainly—esthetic fascination with great force working darkly over great weakness. We are back in Hogarth's world, which *uses* without much subtlety or ambiguity that same fascination, and uses it to help the victim to find allies in the real world of history.

Cassy had lost her children, and thereby all her reasons for wanting freedom for herself; she prepared and performed her scenario only to bring Emmeline to freedom. Harriet Beecher Stowe was a white woman born in Connecticut. She wrote her book, of course, not to save herself from slavery, but to save others. It seems clear that she was moved to write *Uncle Tom's Cabin* by many experiences and eyewitness accounts, but also by the passing of the Fugitive Slave Law of 1850, which made it compulsory for any person finding a runaway slave to return him to his owner. She was an ally of the victims of that essentially cruel relationship, and was angered by the legal action that would adroitly empty America of all the slave's allies.

One of the important similarities between Mrs. Stowe and Cassy is this: the total victim is shown by her actions to be not always alone. That victim may be helped to her feet, to action, by others—if these others can see her and can get to her, and if the allies themselves have the force of passion and of intellect to upset or escape the hierarchy of power.

We are now ready to discuss an example of cruelty in history. But before doing so, let us consider the line of argument we have been pursuing. In the Hogarth chapter we saw cruelty as being not simply a matter of inflicting pain; we saw it as involving a destructive power-relationship between persons. In Hogarth's engravings that power-relationship is ultimately terminated— usually by the death of the victimizer under the stable power of the law. In the chapter on Sade, we saw the same relationship between the victimizer and the victim, but this time the disparity between the vigor of the villain and the passivity of his victim is so great that the power-relationship cannot be terminated by society or any individuals. The cruel moment is as insulated from consequences as the victim of it is from the outside world. The joy of doing something execrable without any hindrance, the joy of exerting, in that moment, one's power absolutely, perfectly, is exemplified and praised by Sade. He imagines away any hindrance to that exertion of power because he shares with Hogarth the belief that obstacles hinder cruelty, at least when those obstacles become great enough. And in sharing this belief with Hogarth, he confirms one of the basic points of this book, that cruelty is indeed a matter of power, whatever else it may be: when the exertion of power is substantially hindered, then cruelty is hindered. Sade wants to maximize that power in order to enjoy, at least in the imagination, the titillating irritations of crushing feeble resistances, and so he imagines castles and other impregnable situations, inhabited by physically and mentally vigorous creatures smashing physically and mentally passive ones.

But if the power of his vigorous beings is great, the power of the Gothic villain is even greater, or at least *looks* even greater. Melmoth can overcome obstacles of space, time, and materiality, and so can Dracula, and Peter Quint (in *The Turn of the Screw*). There is something vast and indefinite, something "totally other" than our everyday experience in the power of the great Gothic villains, something so massive and extraordinary as to be fascinating to us and to his victims.

But there is one power even the Gothic villain, and presumably his master the Devil, does not have: it is power over the minds of his victims. Every victim mentally resists her victimizer, and ultimately avoids the temptation to become totally passive under him, mind and body. This mental resistance even Sade recognized in the "dissertations" that were held by his victimizers and victims between physical tortures. No vigorous spirit ever convinces his victim that Sadism is "natural." But for Sade the physical exertion of power was the main desideratum, and so his "strong beings" are successes, despite their failures to convince their victims. In the Gothic Tale, which is involved with spiritual, usually religious, matters, physical smashing is not the consummation of cruelty—only succumbing to temptation would be such a consummation. But this fall never comes, and so, as in Hogarth's pictured morals, the villain "pays," is himself victimized by the victim and her allies (including God Himself). As in Hogarth, the consequences of cruelty are important, and they are important because the victim has allies and has herself spiritual powers that keep her from being smashed with impunity.

The Gothic dualisms of mind and body or apparent power and real power are, however, not as important to us as the fact they illustrate: the victim, though physically powerless compared with the villain, may be spiritually or mentally powerful compared to him, and the spiritual resistance she offers limits his power and eventually helps terminate it.

We are now ready to consider an example in history that will develop and confirm these ideas—insofar as such broad ideas can be confirmed by facts. In turning to history, we shall be discussing what Harriet Beecher Stowe called a "system" and its power, not an individual villain and his power. Art—except, perhaps for the "art" of Harriet Beecher Stowe—handles the power of persons more effectively than it does the power of systems. We have taken advantage of this until now. Now we must turn to the indefinite power of organized society, of the "compact majority." We must see how it exerts its cruelties, and how—or whether—its victims exert their powers against it.

THE BLACK PEOPLE AND GROCERIES

THE scene is the concentration camp at Auschwitz, in July of 1942. The prisoners in the camp are standing behind their Nazi leaders waiting for Heinrich Himmler to arrive for an inspection tour (italics mine):

> In the tenth row outside our Block, the Block Senior found Yankel Meisel without his full quota of tunic buttons.
> It took some seconds for the enormity of the crime to sink in. Then he felled him with a blow. . . . I saw the Block Senior, with two of his helpers, hauling Yankel inside the barrack block.
> Out of sight, they acted like men who have been shamed and betrayed will act. They beat and kicked the life out of him. They pummelled him swiftly, frantically, trying to blot him out, to sponge him from the scene and from their minds; and Yankel, who had forgotten to sew his buttons on, had not even the good grace to die quickly and quietly.
> He screamed. It was a strong, querulous scream, ragged in the hot, still air. Then it turned suddenly to the thin, plaintive wail of abandoned bagpipes, but it did not fade so fast. It went on and on and on, flooding the vacuum of silence, snatching at tightly-reined minds and twisting them with panic, rising even above the ugly thump of erratic blows. *At that moment, I think, we all hated Yankel Meisel, the little old Jew who was spoiling everything, who was causing trouble for us all with his long, lone, futile protest.*[1]

A few pages later in *I Cannot Forgive* the attitude of Yankel Meisel's fellow prisoners toward his crime and punishment is summarized in an image: what Yankel did was "to drop his tiny personal grain of sand into the smooth machinery."[2]

We have been seeing cruelty "writ large" in works of art,

93

the way Plato studied justice writ large in his ideal Republic. And the main image that emerged from our study was that of a castle, a fortress in which victims can be isolated from all help or escape, so that they can be smashed by the established lord of the castle. A concentration camp was such a castle during the Third Reich, but we are going to continue our study by discussing American cruelty, and we shall see that cruelty writ large in a broader set of pictures than we have been using—images that include machinery and the grains of sand that men drop into them.

The maiming and destruction of men can be done in various ways. Victimization for Sade was something a "strong being" did to a weaker one mainly for erotic stimulation. His heroes needed bloody victims in order to get tumescent. And, like orgasms, Sade's cruelties were episodic; they consisted of one cruel event after another with no connection between them. As we have seen in Chapter Two, his cruelties involved no consequences as far as punishment or even resistance against the "vigorous spirit" is concerned. The locus of his cruelties was always the moment, a particular time in which the flesh and will of the strong being were colliding with a particular victim, just to keep the "vital juices" of the strong being boiling.

But these collisions were not only with particular victims— they were for Sade collisions with the laws and customs of society. Sade flourished in the eighteenth century when both ecclesiastical and secular authorities were crumbling. The *Philosophes* helped undermine the Church, and in the end that victim-king Louis XVI got his head chopped off. Collision with the establishment was the order (or disorder) of the day as it is for many people in America now. Sade more than any other Frenchman of his century wanted to collide with the public order, with all public order. His heroes' vital juices boiled best not simply because they were colliding with and smashing particular victims; they boiled best because they were colliding with common sense, common morality, common religion. They boiled most vigorously when they were being *perverse*, when they were contradicting the established ways for the sheer joy of contradicting them. Throughout Sade's main writings you read injunctions like "Delivering ourselves ceaselessly up to our most monstrous desires."[3]

The heart of perversity is paradox for the sake of irritation; you should do exactly what you shouldn't do, and you should do it only because collision with the public wisdom is the best way of keeping your self from the death-in-life of cowardly, practical, anesthetic habit. Edgar Allan Poe in his little essay "The Imp of the Perverse" gives us the best analysis of perversity I know; and he gives us a short version of this analysis in "The Black Cat" when he writes:

> ... the spirit of PERVERSENESS. Of this spirit philosophy takes no account. Yet I am not more sure that my soul lives, than I am that perverseness is one of the primitive impulses of the human heart ... which give direction to the character of Man. Who has not, a hundred times, found himself committing a vile or a stupid action, for no other reason than because he knows he should *not*? Have we not a perpetual inclination, in the teeth of our best judgment, to violate that which is *Law*, merely because we understand it to be such? ... this unfathomable longing of the soul *to vex itself*—to offer violence to its own nature—to do wrong for the wrong's sake only. .... [4]

But Sadean cruelty has another aspect, aside from its episodic, perverse nature, an aspect expressed in the last part of the passage I have quoted from Poe's "The Black Cat": *self*-irritation. The blasé Marquis was interested in stimulating his own sensibilities by satisfying what Poe called "the unfathomable longing of the soul *to vex itself* ...." In the chapter on Sade we noticed that the imagination had an immense role to play in his notion of cruelty: the Sadean Strong Beings, the Noirceuils, the Saint-Fonds, the Juliettes, were creatures protected by Sade's imagining away of all resistances; whatever irritations they got from slashing or smashing their victims arose from their own and Sade's perverse pleasure in doing what was wrong without any solid resistances from the external world. Collision, in the sense of real and fatal collision that harmed *them* did not occur; or if it did, it occurred in their imaginations, in their own consciousnesses, and did not actually harm them. In short, Sade's victims never struck back, had no reality as resistances. Living in the subjective moment, Sade and his heroes and heroines lived for self-gratification by self-irritation.

To live episodically, passionately, irritatingly is quite different from living practically, as we noticed in the chapter on Sade. The practical man is the man who thinks efficiently in terms of long-range success, happiness, wealth. Socially acceptable goals are what he is after, and the means he devises to reach these goals must also be socially acceptable. Practical wisdom for Aristotle, and for many philosophers after him, is the governance of our impulses by a clear insight into means and ends; it is the capacity to bring order, long-range regularity, and success, into a life that is too often chaotic, full of short-range passions that ignore the "golden mean" between too much and too little. Practical wisdom is common sense in the service of common mores, and Sade's kind of cruelty is the total enemy of common sense.

But there is a kind of destruction or maiming that fits rather neatly into common sense or "practical wisdom." It is the maiming that is going on in that first plate of Hogarth's *Marriage:* the fathers are seeking respectability on the one hand and money on the other (with its kind of respectability); and they are reasoning quite logically from means to ends when they are using their children to attain these ends. Destruction is frequently consistent with common sense. And when this is the case, the destruction itself is a necessary means to a very important end—or the means is not even seen to be destructive. As we have noticed, those fathers have turned their faces away from their children now; they are thinking about their own ends and how to attain them. And when they think of these they find it quite possible, one feels sure, to brush aside any objections on the part of their children with the paternal assertion that father knows best. Father is more practically wise than they—he sees the long run, and they, children that they are, are confined myopically in the moment, in fleeting passions of disgust or boredom with each other, etc.

And so we have noticed two kinds of victimization: overt and covert, violent and peaceful, perverse and common-sensical. But though we have found the distinction worth making, and worth seeing writ large in the works of Hogarth and Sade, we have tried to keep our eye on a fact too often ignored in treatments of cruelty—that the victim of both sorts is just as maimed when he is harmed common-sensically as he is when he is harmed perversely. Those two young people whose lives are smashed in the last plates of the *Marriage* are no less ruined than is Ann Gill in the third plate of Hogarth's *Cruelty* engravings, even though Tom Nero harmed her perversely (the way he hurt those animals). Those two fathers harmed their children common-sensically, but they harmed them unto death. The distinction between Sadism and practical harm-doing is worth making, but it is not the main distinction of this book as far as the victim's awareness is concerned.

Our main distinction between cruelties has been suggested at the beginning of the Sade chapter. Sade refused to condemn aristocratic prisoners brought before him during the Reign of Terror while he sat on the tribunal of the *Section des Piques;* and he refused because cruelty for him was a personal matter, a matter between individuals, not between individuals and the state with its cold, abstract legalities. The only reason for killing was in the moment itself: it was that feeling one has *now*, when one smashes another creature. States and their laws are dead abstractions compared to the hot passions of an individual; his mental and physical *boiling* is the only valid "defense" for murder; in fact, excitement is the only valid criterion for judging the value of anything in life.

But cold-blooded, impersonal, institutionalized harm-doing is something that has only conventional, empty, abstract reasons to support it. Capital punishment is in league with all those artificial devices men have made to keep from being hot with passion, natural. And it is this way of doing harm that is the main topic of this chapter.

Systematic or institutional cruelty can, like personal cruelty, be covert or overt, peaceful or violent. Most colonial empires were created or at least maintained by terror and destruction done for the sake of the Manifest Destiny or glory of the imperialist power. And Yankel Meisel himself was at the moment of his beating a victim of violent institutional cruelty (with, perhaps, some admixture of personal cruelty). Of course Sade's advocacy of personal violent victimization was deeply different from these sorts of violent harm-doing; he was advocating person-to-person individualistic harm for the sheer joy of hurting.

Imperialist wars or concentration camps have something

shared by all institutional cruelties—a public rationale, a purpose that at least British or American or French or Dutch or German imperialists could understand and accept. Hitler's *Mein Kampf* is such a rationale, and so are various versions of the White Man's Burden theme in Western thought. Institutionalized cruelty always has a public logic—this is part of what it means to act institutionally.

But institutional *covert*, quiet cruelty is of all the modes of maiming that we have been discussing the *most elusive for its victims*, and therefore the most important for this book. All cruelty is a "terrible crushing and grinding" (as the playwright-philosopher Antonin Artaud put it), but this kind of harm-doing happens with machine-like efficiency; it moves slowly, uneventfully, like a quiet, well-oiled mechanism. In fact, it functions so smoothly that both the people who control it and the people who suffer in it often do not know that there is any other way for life to go. People get used to it, and when they have cause to question it, their victimizers and themselves can bring forth many reasons for its necessity. It becomes, both in men's habits and in their rational defenses, a natural, and sometimes even a divine necessity.

As we have often noticed, cruelty is not simply the causing and suffering of pain—it is the maiming of a life, whether or not that life happens to feel any dramatic physical pain at the time it is being maimed. Dramatic pain is episodic, and is certainly always involved with *violent* cruelties, both personal and institutional: Tom Nero's Ann Gill felt such pain while he was slitting her throat; Tom Nero, Hogarth seems to want us to believe, felt pain during his institutionally cruel execution (and even perhaps— *mirabile dictu*—while his corpse was being mutilated). But there are times when covert institutional cruelty does not reveal itself in dramatic moments of physical pain. Its victims might be vaguely, indefinitely uncomfortable, or they might be convinced by the institutional rationale, or they might be habituated to their maiming, or they might learn to disregard it and turn their attention elsewhere. But still that institutional mechanism will be grinding them slowly and exceeding small.

These fellow prisoners of Yankel Meisel were such accommodating victims of undramatic cruelty. And they showed it by hating Yankel Meisel while he was being pounded to death inside the barrack; they showed it by believing that "The little old Jew . . . was spoiling everything . . . causing trouble for us all . . . ." True, there were episodes of overt cruelty; true they were imprisoned; but everything was going smoothly—and then they had their dreams of freedom. Besides, this man dropped "his tiny personal grain of sand into the smooth machinery." The sin that appalled them was the sin of inefficiency, the sin of breaking the smooth pace of the machine that was maiming and destroying them all. What they wanted above all—at least during that episode—was to be inspected and approved by the man whose task it was to exterminate them all and who had already exterminated many of their co-prisoners.

And the fact that this can happen in the minds of the victims of institutional, covert cruelty makes this kind of cruelty the most subtle kind of cruelty one can study if one is studying cruelty from the point of the view of its victim. If the victim is feeling no violent physical pain while the machines grind him, if his own destruction is something *he* wants to go smoothly, efficiently, if he is *fascinated* (to use our word from the chapter on the Gothic Tale), by the smoothness and power of the machine, it would seem that there is little hope for him.

There is another factor that makes institutional cruelty especially dangerous: it is perpetrated by a power far greater than the power of any single person, and therefore the victim runs immense risks of being destroyed when he tries to evade or resist it. As Frantz Fanon puts it in *The Wretched of the Earth*,

> . . . colonialism is not a thinking machine, nor a body endowed with reasoning faculties. It is violence in its natural state. . . . [5]

And this domination of the weak by the strong is in the hands of leaders and followers possessing great military and economic power. The risk of resisting or escaping such powerful men constantly reminds the victims that, as Fanon puts it, they are "encircled . . . fragile and in permanent danger . . . ."[6] These immense risks cooperate with psychological forces that we have summarized by the term *fascinosum* to hinder resistance to the destructive institution. One's life seems so fragile under the threats of that great force; and yet, degraded as it is, it is all one has, and is better than death. To think expediently, because of the danger, and hypnotically, because of the fascination, is a great temptation for the victim of institutional cruelty. And in those moments when the fascination fails, the strongest temptation of all appears: the temptation of despair, expressed in the line from "Ole Man River": "I'm tired of livin', and feared of dyin'."

Moreover, in a situation of institutional cruelty, the powerful group can protect and even condone acts of personal cruelty by individuals who happen to belong to that group. This is not a point that Sade considered, but it is of vital importance for any study of cruelty in history. Not only can covert institutional cruelty readily degenerate into naked violence on the part of the powerful group, but it can generate and protect the cruelties of individuals towards individuals. The stories of the concentration camps are not only stories of mass murders; they are stories of individual actions, like the smashing of a child's head against a wall, or the spade-killing of an old woman who was doing no harm. These individual actions, cruelties of a bloody or of a bloodless sort, are not ordered from above—they are not even always called for by a given situation. They are perpetrated because the victimizers were a part of the powerful group, felt like perpetrating them for Sadean or other reasons, and were able to perpetrate them with impunity because of the uncontested power their group possessed.

In short, the destruction that institutional cruelty spawns is not always institutionalized destruction, and so the two sorts of harm-doing are by no means separate. In fact, a plausible defense could be made for the claim that an institution never kills—it is always an individual who does this. But in this broad study we cannot explore these subtleties: all we are trying to see are the main forms that cruelty takes, the kinds of situations in which mortal harm-doing occurs; we are not trying to blame or praise groups or individuals as much as we are trying to make distinctions that help us to understand the nature of cruelty. The fact is that victimizers sometimes share a "cause" and an established set of laws and practices as well as the power to work their wills on the minds and bodies of others, and such powerful establishments destroy their victims not perversely and not even absent-mindedly: they destroy them on principle and often with public pride. The cruelty of Sade or of Hogarth's Tom Nero is importantly different from the cruelty exhibited in the following remark, made with regard to the Protestant religious wars in France during the sixteenth century:

> I personally heard the proposition made and defended by a well-known Catholic . . . that there was less danger [in the hereafter] by eating a child, in such circumstances [during the siege of Paris by the Protestant Henry of Navarre], than by recognizing [supporting] a heretic . . . and that all the best theologians of the University were of this opinion.[7]

What this distinction means in terms of our paradox of cruelty is that institutional cruelty does its best to conceal the prong of the paradox that finds mortal maiming disgusting and unjustifiable. Institutional cruelty is a public, often vastly powerful form of the pragmatic cruelty we saw in the first plate of Hogarth's *Marriage,* wherein those fathers had their backs turned to their victims and their minds directed to money and to "honor." Institutional cruelty does everything it can to conceal the fact that it is destroying its victims, and in doing this it keeps its spectators from feeling disgust and from being confused by the paradox of trying to justify the unjustifiable, of trying to praise the smashing of the weak.

Institutional cruelty insulates one prong of the paradox from the other, keeps one hand from knowing what the other hand is doing, and it does this by using at least two devices: secrecy, and rigid abstraction. The Nazis, for instance, had "bearers of secrets"[8] who alone knew about the planned extermination of the Jews; and to facilitate the keeping of these secrets they had a "language rule" (*Sprachregelung*) that kept ordinary people from knowing when they were talking or writing about killing Jews. According to this rule, instead of using words like "killing" or "extermination" they used phrases like "Final Solution" (*Endlösung*) of "the Jewish question." And physical secrecy was valuable: great efforts were made to keep the people from knowing what was going on in those concentration camps. In American forms of institutional cruelty, secrecy was maintained by isolated plantations, and later by xenophobic little communities that jealously concealed from the outside world any facts about the way they treated their black people.

The other important device for covering up or preventing man's disgust with human destruction is the rigid abstraction, the word used to refer to the victim, but used in a way that makes that victim a creature from another species, and a creature without individuality or personality. "Nigger" was such a word in America, and *Jude* or "Jew" became such a word in Nazi Germany. Using such a verbal device, the victimizer-institution could destroy its victims almost absent-mindedly, without seeing that it was smashing individual human beings.

In our chapter on Sade we saw that he had his own devices for avoiding disgust and maximizing the desire for smashing human beings: he tried to make cruelty "natural," and he made his victims esthetic objects, dancing to the music of their pain, not individual resisting persons. But Sade's pleasure in cruelty came from perverseness, specifically from the paradox of cruelty. He required "irritation" or scandal, frankly sought to *violate* conventional morality, public custom, all those forces—including the law—that condemned mortal maiming as disgusting. Institutional cruelty does not trade mainly in irritation or perverseness, in episodes of subjective stimulation, in short-term pleasures-in-pain. It trades in long-term efficiency, the smooth operation of power with a minimum of conflict or paradox. It is practical; it gets things done in the long run—or at least this is what it tries to do. It seeks efficiency, not self-indulgence. It is an expression of that view of life we distinguished from the "Existential" in the chapter on Sade—the Pragmatical view of life.

And so, instead of subjective, episodic self-irritation through paradox it offers publicly acceptable, conventional ideals like the purification of the German Nation, the attainment of Heaven, and, in the case of the Southern planters, the profitable use of one's own property—both animate and inanimate, both human and non-human. Above all it seeks smooth, long-term, public efficiency, a way of exerting its power without ambivalence in the victim or in his sympathizers.

And so personal, perverse cruelty faces the paradox, faces *both* man's desire for and man's disgust with the smashing of human life, and faces them more candidly than does institutional cruelty, with all its devices for covering up the particular face and force of the victim. Perverse cruelty may use devices like those of Sade to soften the paradox, but it does not erect such elaborate precautions for concealing the destruction of individual human beings as does institutional cruelty. After all, Sade describes the maimings, often in great detail, and takes as much pleasure in the description of them as his victimizers take in the. perpetration of them.

And so if we accept the assumption of Hogarth's engravings and of this book that mortal cruelty, the "terrible waste of life," is something to be avoided, institutional cruelty is the most dangerous of all the kinds of cruelty we have been studying. It is dangerous not simply because of the numbers of victims involved, nor simply because the power of the victimizer is so great relative to each of his victims, but also because institutional cruelty can *veil* our precious disgust with the destruction of human life, and can secure the consent of large numbers of "ordinary," "decent" people—including the victims themselves.

We could try to specify the nature of institutional cruelty by continuing to study the Nazi concentration camps, but we shall not do so for various reasons. At the time of this writing, the camps are no longer functioning, though some of their causes and some of their effects still operate in men's minds and bodies. Still, the visible institutions are gone, and the psychological and sociological impact of them is now too diffuse to give clarity to our macroscopic explication of cruelty. Survivors of the concentration camps are talking about past victimizations, when they choose to talk about them at all; they feel the effects of those past victimizations, the wounds, but they are no longer being actually victimized by those camps. Jews are no longer victims writ large and they are not expressing to us the victim's awareness in all of its immediacy.

Moreover, I am an American, and separated by differences in language and culture from the minds of the Nazis. To write large this elusive kind of cruelty it seems reasonable to study a kind of institutional cruelty known to me and felt by me as intimately as possible. Moreover, it seems reasonable that if I would plead the cause of the victim I should myself be implicated in the institution I am examining—either as a victim or as a victimizer.

Ever since that day in 1619 when a Dutch slave ship brought the first twenty black people to our shores as slaves, America has institutionalized a kind of cruelty so massive, so long in its history, so destructive in its effects that anyone who would see institutional cruelty writ large could study that institution with profit. And more importantly, the victims of it are still being victimized by it, and are expressing their reactions now in many media, and abundantly.

From the beginning slave traders called their African cargo *negros* or "blacks," and both these words *meant* "slaves." The three words were synonymous. In 1740 the state of South Carolina passed legislation that provided that

> . . . all negroes . . . mulattoes, or mestizos, who are or shall here-
> after be in the province, and all their issue and offspring, born or
> to be born, shall be and they are hereby declared to be and remain
> forever hereafter absolute slaves . . . [9]

And the same provision obtained in Georgia and Mississippi, as well as, implicitly, in other Southern states in the eighteenth and the nineteenth centuries. And so the main words that referred to black people labelled them—in the act of referring to them— "absolute slaves."

Since the beginning of history men have been brought by

force into bondage, but the bondage of the American slave was, even when it was not painful, amongst the most "absolute" in the world's history. To see what this means, compare American slavery with Spanish slavery as far as the law is concerned. *Las Siete Partidas* of Spain (and many of its colonies) provided that the slave could: (1) marry in the church and stay with his wife and children, (2) testify against the master about ill-treatment, and (3) be freed upon earning and paying his master a fixed sum or upon denouncing a forced rape against a virgin or upon becoming the guardian of the master's children, etc. In short, there was in Spain and elsewhere a contractual arrangement between the master and the slave; though the relationship originated in force, the slave could act effectively against or despite his master's will.[10]

But in America the slave was sheer chattel, animate property. He was not a party to a contract—he was in "absolute" slavery. That is, in most slave states he could not use marriage as grounds for staying with his family; his family was made up of movable pieces of property, separable at the will of the master, without any recourse on the part of the slave. His testimony against his master was ruled out; no matter what his master did to him, he could not respond before the law. Finally, there was the issue of manumission. As Tannenbaum points out in *Slave and Citizen* manumission is "the crucial element in slavery; it implies the judgment on the moral status of the slave, and foreshadows his role in case of freedom."[11] When it is readily available to the slave, and when it is safe and sure once obtained, the slave is not presumed to be in a slave *caste*. In most Southern states in America it was in practice impossible for a slave to obtain his own manumission by his own labors, and it was in most states equally difficult for others to obtain his freedom.[12] In most states a freed slave could be enslaved again for minor infractions of the law or could have his manumission papers torn up for no legal reasons, and could be sold at auction by any white man he happened to encounter. To be black meant to be a slave, unless you could prove you were free—and this proof could be torn up before your eyes.

Scholars have disputed the horrors of slavery (as late as 1918

Ulrich B. Phillips argued for its prevalent benignity), but that dispute has subsided with the mountainous accumulation of evidence for horrors both violent and quiet. Josiah Henson (Harriet Beecher Stowe's prototype for Uncle Tom) tells in his *Story* how his father was punished for protecting his mother from rape by an overseer: he was lashed one hundred times on the bare skin until he could barely groan.

> His head was then thrust against the post, and his right ear fastened to it with a tack; a swift pass of a knife, and the bleeding member was left sticking to the place. Then came a hurra from the degraded crowd, and the exclamation, "That's what he's got for striking a white man."[13]

Perhaps Wilbur J. Cash in his classic *The Mind of the South* has most sharply summarized the evidence for the painful aspects of slavery:

> The lash lurked always in the background. Its open crackle could often be heard where field hands were quartered. Into the gentlest houses drifted now and then the sound of dragging chains and shackles, the bay of hounds, the report of pistols on the trail of the runaway. And, as the advertisements of the time incontestably prove, mutilation and the mark of the branding iron were pretty common.[14]

Though there were many gentle masters and happy houses, Cash goes on,

> ... the institution was brutalizing—to white men—virtually unlimited power acted inevitably to call up, in the coarser sort of master, that sadism which lies concealed in the depths of universal human nature—bred angry impatience and a taste for cruelty for its own sake, with a strength that neither the kindliness I have so often referred to (it continued frequently to exist unimpaired side by side, and in the same man, with this other) nor notions of honor could effectually restrain. And in the common whites it bred a savage and ignoble hate for the Negro, which required only opportunity to break forth in relentless ferocity.[15]

And so it was true that institutional cruelty, decorous or violent, was by no means *separate* from personal cruelties—in fact it helped bring them about. Slavery was a vast heap of all sorts of cruelties, personal and public, violent and quiet.

But to emphasize these symptoms, dramatic as they may be, is to give way to sentiment. Our curiosity regarding the pains of cruelty must not keep us from achieving an insight into the human relationship that is the very center of victimization. As we have noticed, Harriet Beecher Stowe put that relationship in one way when she wrote at the end of *Uncle Tom's Cabin:* "There is, actually, nothing to protect the slave's life, but the *character* of the master."[16] And what this means is that the slave is utterly passive in relation to his master. If "negro" or "black" (or "mulatto") means "slave" and if "non-negro" or "white" means "master" or "mister" then blacks are utterly passive by virtue of being black, under the wills of whites, who have the legal right and the actual power to be active. Not the slave's own will, not his own talents, not his own knowledge, not his own arm can in the long run protect him—only "the master," only the white man. He is in the danger, the dominion of the whites, by virtue of being black, by virtue of wearing the unremovable badge of servitude. *He* makes no difference in this fundamental relationship; *he* cannot resist effectively in a relationship that is not a contract between individuals but an absolute domination of the strong over the weak. He is the victim of the active, deciding individuals because he is a member of a caste. And he is in this condition not by virtue of any individual weakness in his own flesh or mind; he is in this condition not because he did or did not do anything. He is there independently of his own will or lack of will, independently of any of his particular characteristics; he is there because powerful *others* have managed to make all people with a certain shade of skin "absolute slaves," as absolutely passive as one can make a human being short of killing him biologically.

The center of slavery is simple, and may be seen in this advertisement in the *New Orleans Bee:*

> NEGROES FOR SALE.——A Negro woman, 24 years of age, and her two children, one eight and the other three years old. Said negroes will be sold SEPARATELY or together, *as desired.* The woman is a good seamstress. She will be sold low for cash, or EXCHANGED FOR GROCERIES.
>
> For terms, apply to MATTHEW BLISS & CO., 1 Front Levee[17]

People, not by virtue of their individual weaknesses or strengths, are put in the position of being as passive as groceries. When they are "good" they are good by the white master's standards for chattel, and their highest goals must be to satisfy his standards, the way a hard-working mule is a good mule or the way good groceries are good to be eaten. Utter passivity, in total independence of individual traits, under the will of the white man—this was American slavery.

In order to maintain this essentially cruel relationship, America became one of the most elaborate and extensive networks of castles in history. It had to isolate each victim in the victimizer's dominion. African blacks were first captured (often by other blacks), and then sold to traders who sent them on the infamous Middle Passage across the Atlantic, with all the horrors of tight confinement, rotten food, stench, disease, death—all permeated with their sense of loss and unknowing. Next there was the brutal "seasoning" period for the survivors; and after this, there was slavery itself on the tobacco, indigo, rice, and later, cotton plantations.

We have noticed how the law made the black person helpless, without recourse, and with no—or little—possibility of escaping his unselving. The plantations, like Legree's, were isolated from each other and were under the domain of the planter, and of the planter alone. Up to now we have been dealing with fictional castles; let us consider a real one, as described in the autobiography of the Negro Abolitionist Frederick Douglass. Even in the comparatively enlightened state of Maryland, his plantation was

> . . . seldom visited by a single ray of healthy public sentiment, where slavery, wrapt in its own congenial darkness, could and did develop all its malign and shocking characteristics, where it could be indecent without shame, cruel without shuddering, and murderous without apprehension of fear of exposure or punishment. Just such a secluded dark, and out-of-the-way place was the home plantation of Colonel Edward Lloyd, in Talbot County, Eastern Shore of Maryland. It was far away from all the great

thoroughfares of travel and commerce, and proximate to no town or village. There was neither schoolhouse nor townhouse in its neighborhood. . . . The overseer's children went off somewhere in the state to school, and therefore could bring no foreign or dangerous influence from abroad to embarrass the natural operation of the slave system of the place.[18]

Everything, including the slaves themselves, was owned by Colonel Lloyd. It was

. . . a little nation by itself, having its own . . . rules, regulations, and customs. The troubles and controversies arising there were not settled by the civil power of the State. The overseer was the important dignitary. He was generally accuser, judge, jury, advocate, and executioner. The criminal was always dumb, and no slave was allowed to testify other than against his brother slave.[19]

There was, in short, no defense for the black people, from without or from within, and there was no getting away. No wonder then that Douglass says that "It resembled, in some respects, descriptions I have since read of the old baronial domains in Europe . . . ."[20] In most plantations the planter was helped by poor white "patrols," dogs, and many other animate parts of the castle wall.

But the wall was not only physical. It was a crime to teach slaves to read and write in most Southern states, and so the blacks who arrived cut off from their tribal and personal past were kept trapped and passive in their new home by being unable to read. House and field slaves alike were totally the property, totally within the danger of the planter, as physically and mentally sequestered as any slaves in the history of the world.

The Emancipation Proclamation of 1863 and the victory for the North that followed cracked the castle walls and spilled out the freedmen. But the catastrophic death later in the nineteenth century of both the Freedmen's Bureau and the repository of the freedmen's money, the Freedmen's Bank, institutions that could have done so much to free the black man from impotent poverty, these deaths issued in a new pattern of castles.[21] Black men were for the greater part in the region where they had been slaves; invaders had freed them, and the freedom of the blacks from the old laws of slavery was for Southern Americans a galling reminder of defeat by an alien power. Blacks were still blacks, that is, slaves—the words men used still had their old meanings; and so new ways of isolating and rendering passive had to be devised. One of these devices was already at hand—the local administration of justice, with local juries and elected judges, and the tradition of the rights of the states to decide their own destinies as autonomously as is consistent with the life of the United States. The judges, the public prosecutors, the sheriffs, the chiefs of police, all were dependent upon the vote of the local majority, the whites. And of course they expressed the prejudices of that majority. These prejudices kept the Negro a passive victim of white power, a domesticated animal. The democratic mechanisms of the law made the freed black people as powerless as the old aristocratic slave mechanisms had done, and the castle walls were not less impregnable for being less visible on statute books. The pressure of an isolated community upon its blacks to keep them from getting "uppity" or "smart" took the place of slavery, and every white man's gaze (as well as the gaze of accommodating blacks) became part of the glittering eyes of the powerful white master, now no longer a master in name.

And all the local laws and law-enforcement agencies that functioned "to keep the Negro in his place"[22] were buttressed not only by the solidarity of the whites, who kept court cases from getting up to the often more just Federal courts, but also by xenophobia, the white man's fear and hatred of "strangers" and "outside agitators." Anyone who might try to penetrate that place and "give the niggers ideas" was an invader of the castle and was treated as such.

At this point in our account, it is useful to warn the reader that the economic, political, psychological, and other forces at work at this—and at any other—time are so complex as to be inexhaustible. Again and again Gunnar Myrdal in his massive, classic study of the Negro in America, warns us of "The perplexities and manifoldness of the Negro problem . . . ."[23] He tells us that there is a "cumulative causation" involving many, sometimes independent, factors that created this history of the black people, and he warns us—and himself—that we are simplifying in any account we give. But Myrdal still finds a "unity" in that history, what he calls a "system" of forces (economic, political, etc.) all involved with "white discrimination."[24] We have been finding such unity under the rubrics of isolation and passivity, but this unity admittedly is a result of flying rather high over the many complex facts, and seeing only outlines.

Let us take one more step in tracing the way America helped the essential relationship of slavery to continue, prolonged the shadow of slavery across our history and our minds. The step takes us to the turn of the nineteenth century and the first part of the twentieth: the Jim Crow laws.[25] At first against the desires of some influential Southerners, there was institutionalized the intimate and public insult of separate toilets, restaurants, churches, common carriers (like trains and buses), and schools. Quietly, blacks were ordered *for no particular, avowed reason—* except a reason-less law—to use "separate but equal" physical, mental, and spiritual facilities. Their black skin *was no overtly recognized reason* for not being permitted to use these facilities. What does the *color of one's skin* have to do—except in the minds of those who think of Negroes as slaves—with one's place of eating or of being educated? Payment of the fare is relevant to one's presence on a bus; an ability to pay the bill is relevant to being permitted to eat in a restaurant; being a citizen is relevant to allowing one's children to attend certain schools. But no reason was relevant to keeping blacks out of these institutions or facilities. No reason except the *implicit* one that the blacks were inferior, unworthy of white company, and passive, powerless enough to be excluded for no defended purpose. The white man's will was the black man's law.

The Plessy *v.* Ferguson Supreme Court decision of 1896 greatly encouraged the proliferation of Jim Crow laws. Plessy, who had one-eighth Negro blood, tried to sit in a train coach reserved for whites. He was ordered by the conductor to sit in the coach for Negroes; he refused and was arrested on the charge of violating Louisiana's "separate but equal" accommodations statute. In deciding on the constitutionality of that statute the Supreme Court said that the Fourteenth Amendment, which gave all men equal privileges and immunities under the law, was being complied with when you gave black people "separate but equal" use of trains and buses. But the insult had become law mainly by state and municipal legislation, not by Supreme Court action. In fact, the meaning of the Plessy *v.* Ferguson decision was not only that it made equality consistent with enforced segregation; it was also that the Supreme Court bowed respectfully in the direction of those local machines, the states and cities, with their "established usages, customs, and traditions" that made the Negro's very flesh ineligible for contact with white flesh, except on the white man's degrading terms. That decision told those castle-machines to keep on grinding the black man exceeding small.

But you must understand the physical and mental torture involved in Jim Crowism not only in terms of slinking into alleys to urinate or crossing great distances to find a place to eat or to live when you are surrounded by restaurants and hotels; you must understand this intimate insult in another way. The way has to do with slavery. One of the issues in the Plessy *v.* Ferguson decision was whether the Thirteenth Amendment to the Constitution had anything to do with Plessy's being ordered by a train conductor to sit in a colored coach. The Thirteenth Amendment abolished slavery and all involuntary servitude, except as a result of legally administered punishment for a crime.

The issue covering Jim Crow laws was not simply separation; it was latter-day bondage. The conductor commanded Plessy to go to another car, not because he did not have the right ticket (he had it), but because Negroes were commanded by Whites to seat themselves apart from the Whites: they were commanded in exactly the same spirit that the whole machine of slavery commanded blacks to live in "the street," the slave quarters, or to avoid being "uppity."

To see this more concretely, all we need do is read one of the many accounts Douglass gives in his *Life and Times*—here was segregation operating during and as part of slavery, long before the Plessy case (italics mine):

> My treatment in the use of public conveyances about these times was extremely rough, especially on the Eastern Railroad, from Boston to Portland. On that road, as on many others, there was a mean, dirty, and uncomfortable car set apart for colored trav-

elers called the Jim Crow car. Regarding this as the fruit of slave-holding prejudice and being determined to fight *the spirit of slavery* wherever I might find it, I resolved to avoid this car, though it sometimes required some courage to do so. *The colored people generally accepted the situation and complained of me as making matters worse rather than better by refusing to submit to this proscription.* I, however, persisted, and sometimes was soundly beaten by conductor and brakeman. On one occasion six of these "fellows of the baser sort," under the direction of the conductor, set out to eject me from my seat. As usual, I had purchased a first-class ticket and paid the required sum for it, and on the requirement of the conductor to leave, refused to do so, when he called on these men to "snake me out." They attempted to obey with an air which plainly told me they relished the job. They however found me much attached to my seat, and in removing me I tore away two or three of the surrounding ones, on which I held with a firm grasp, and did the car no service in some other respects. I was strong and muscular, and the seats were not then so firmly attached or of as solid make as now. The result was that Stephen A. Chase, superintendent of the road, ordered all passenger trains to pass through Lynn, where I then lived, without stopping.[26]

When Justice Harlan gave his dissenting opinion in the Plessy Case he put his finger on exactly this fact that involuntary sequestration is "in the spirit of slavery": Jim Crow is the shadow of slavery in men's minds, the shadow of involuntary servitude. Conductors, bus drivers, the crowds, customs, laws, etc., all simply command the Negro to be only where the white man wants him to be. Justice Harlan's dissenting opinion reads:

... in the eye of the law, there is in this country no superior, dominant, ruling class of citizens. There is no caste here. Our Constitution is color-blind. ... The humblest is the peer of the most powerful. ...

The arbitrary separation of citizens, on the basis of race, while they are on a public highway, is a badge of servitude wholly inconsistent with ... civil freedom and ... equality before the law. ... We boast of the freedom enjoyed by our people. ... But it is difficult to reconcile that boast with a state of the law which, practically, puts the brand of servitude and degradation upon a large class of our fellow-citizens.[27]

The Emancipation Proclamation of 1863 did not free the United States of America from the spirit of slavery. The Negro as part of an untouchable (but eminently *usable*) caste is *the* idea of that Louisiana statute about "separate but equal" accommodations. For it is the White Man who commands any Black Man with no regard for his individuality, and gives him no redress before the law when he wishes to flout that command.

Ultimately the insult is this: the color of your skin is the badge of your servitude and your inferiority to us. You are *beneath* our species in a hierarchy of power, sensitivity, and intelligence. But Jim Crow—through a paradox that only *ignoring* the black people could permit to pass unnoticed—created and perpetuated ignorance. For instance, segregated educational facilities made it possible to give much inferior facilities and a far inferior education to black children than were given to white children. Louis R. Harlan, a distant cousin of the dissenting Justice Harlan, has shown in his book *Separate and Unequal* how segregated school facilities produced a swiftly widening gap between black and white education and as he put it "enforced ignorance."[28] C. Vann Woodward said it accurately:

> The Jim Crow laws, unlike feudal laws, did not assign the subordinate group a fixed status in society. They were constantly pushing the Negro farther down.[29]

The black child was left more and more passive, powerless, uneducated compared to the increasing intellectual skills and insights the white child was achieving. This later helped produce the massive emigrations of Negroes from the South, when their menial skills were taken over by machines.

The reasons for this separate and unequal education were various, but amounted to what a certain White Supremacist Clark Howell put thus: " . . . whenever the nigger learns his haec, hoc, he right away forgets all about gee-whoa-buck!"[30] The same reasons that brought slavery to America and kept it here for centuries were the reasons for Jim Crow: the white man needed cheap, steady labor to make an adequate profit. At first it was tobacco, indigo, and rice that required cheap, steady labor, and later, in the deep South, it was King Cotton that required a large, cheap, steady labor force in order to get profits for the white man. Now the situation was more complex, but the white man still wanted the profit, and a passive, obedient creature trapped in intellectual as well as physical ways was useful. Nay, he was even necessary, so used to the good life were some planters and their wives, and so accustomed were all whites, even poor whites, to having passive inferiors no matter how "low" they themselves got in the world.

This is no place to continue the story of the shadow of slavery, the degradation of the black man, the imprisonment of him in ignorant impotence. In the twentieth century the shadow became more subtle while the Jim Crow laws were being dissipated, but to use the words of the greatest sociological thinker the Negro people have produced in America, W.E.B. Du Bois, the black man is still "within the veil" of his skin-color, still separate and inferior, still the victim of arbitrary restrictions in almost every sphere of public and private life.

It is of first importance to see that the separation of white from black facilities is not in itself the primary issue of this chapter. It is the commanding and degrading of black people, rendering them *without recourse* under white commands that constitutes the shadow of slavery. A home is "segregated" from other homes by the will of the homeowner. In such sequestration, which is intimacy, human beings expand and replenish their lives. But when people are trapped by powerful others without escape and without the power of resistance, then victimization is occurring, then men are in *the* cruel relationship, the relationship of unselving, of dependency upon the arbitrary will of a superior being.

All of this is what Harriet Beecher Stowe meant when she said about slavery: "There is actually nothing to protect the slave's life, but the *character* of the master." The slave's own initiative is *nothing*. He is treated as a usable thing, like groceries we may want, and which we eat for our own pleasure as well as to enhance our own power. "Sometimes I feel like I'm almost gone—" is not only a line in a spiritual about motherless children.

On matters of life and death we must try to descend from abstractions as often as possible, or else the great difference between life and death gets covered with clouds. Talking about one's own initiative as "nothing" is conducive to this danger, and also talking of the slave as a useable chattel can involve us in ineffectual abstractions. Finally, in talking about the essential relationship of cruelty as not involving dramatic, episodic pains, we have perhaps gotten so abstract and negative as to be talking to no humane point.

And so let us consider two passages from the autobiographies of two victims, two slaves. The first appears in *Twelve Years a Slave* by Solomon Northup. In that book he talked about the slave's pillow being a stick of wood and his cabin being open to the rain. But these are hardships many poor farmers suffered, and they are not close to the bone of slavery. Consider this passage:

> ... a slave never approaches the gin-house with his basket of cotton but with fear. If it falls short in weight—if he has not performed the full task appointed him, he knows that he must suffer. And if he has exceeded it by ten or twenty pounds, in all probability his master will measure the next day's task accordingly.[31]

We are not confronted here with sadistic tortures—the fears of the slave approaching the gin-house are directed toward an impersonal mechanism, one that tries to get the maximum output from each slave, and does so adroitly. And this dread is spread over all the slave's waking hours:

> It is an offence invariably followed by a flogging, to be found at the quarters after daybreak. Then the fears and labors of another day begin; and until its close there is no such thing as rest. He fears he will be caught lagging through the day; he fears to approach the gin-house with his basket-load of cotton at night; he fears, when he lies down, that he will oversleep himself in the morning. Such is a true, faithful, unexaggerated picture and description of the slave's daily life, during the time of cotton-picking, on the shores of Bayou Boeuf.[32]

Whatever else dread is it is uncertainty concerning one's welfare, uncertainty about someone who can do one harm. That uncertainty about powers that can be destructive is itself destructive of bold action. All those fears throughout the day become a generalized dread of what comes next or of what has power over you. And dread is a kind of paralysis whose object is indefinitely threatening. Dread becomes a way of life, a cringing way that conforms to the purposes of the cotton planter who can make a handsome profit only by rendering his slaves totally passive to his will, in the fields, in their cabins, in his bed, everywhere. Another name for this dreadful uncertainty is "horror." It was felt by the black people under the *mysterium tremendum* of the white machine, as it was felt by the victim of a Gothic agent of Satan.

But the Deep South was one thing, and itself subject to a special dread for slaves; slaves living farther north were often threatened with being sold down the Mississippi River. What of Maryland, and what of a house-slave, whose life was so much more genteel than the field-slave's? To get a hint of the undramatic cruelties of this kind of slavery, consider another passage from the autobiography of Frederick Douglass, who, before he achieved international fame as an Abolitionist orator and advisor to President Lincoln, had had a comparatively fortunate life as a slave. A woman had been whipped:

> The charge against her was very common and very indefinite, namely *"impudence."* This crime could be committed by a slave in a hundred different ways, and depended much upon the temper and caprice of the overseer as to whether it was committed at all. He could create the offense whenever it pleased him. A look, a word, a gesture, accidental or intentional, never failed to be taken as impudence when he was in the right mood for such an offense.[33]

Some masters in most of their moods called a slave "impudent" if he looked his master straight in the eyes.[34] Others were kinder, in most of *their* moods. Now if, as Frederick Douglass said, "the slave must know no higher law than his master's will"[35] and if the force of that "must" is the power of local law-enforcement and of custom, then this highest "law," this will of the master, is always *uncertain* in the slave's mind. People's moods change, and, like the wind, they are not precisely predictable—in fact, they can be massively surprising, especially to a slave who is not privy to the problems in his master's life.

And so the slave is enslaved as much by uncertainty about what is required of him as he is enslaved by specific commands to do specific jobs. And either his life is a life of fearful guesses as to whether he is going to be "impudent" or "uppity" or he lives the life of Douglass's "contented slave" who has retreated into bestial subservience, who has escaped uncertainty by deciding

> . . . to darken his moral and mental vision, and, as far as possible, to annihilate his power of reason. . . .[36]

It was possible for slaves to avoid the uncertainties about this "highest law," his master's will, but the cost of this avoidance ran high: he had to retreat into brutishness, into being, as a man with powers of reasoning and moral judgment, dead while alive.

Having to obey does not in itself make a man a slave. In fact, freedom under the law is a commonplace idea, and has been since the beginning of civilization. But freedom lies in part in man's ability to predict, to know what the law says and how the law will be interpreted and applied. Of course this is not all there is to freedom under the law, but it is an important part of it. The history of freedom under the law is to a very great extent the history of formal procedures that men can know, that men can count upon.

Of course, another aspect of the history of freedom is the opportunity to plead one's case effectively, and this opportunity, as we noticed at the beginning of this chapter, was totally denied the slave, and effectively denied in the many isolated communities in America where lynch law, white juries, elected judges and sheriffs would not accept black testimony in self-defense. But the point here is that certain certainties are necessary for freedom under the law. These certainties are not enough to make a man free (the black man in the nineteenth century knew that if he struck a white man he would in all probability be lynched) but without them, and in a situation where one is not a party to a contract but a passive victim ineligible to testify or plead effectively, the tortures of uncertainty become immense. This is what Douglass meant when he said "It was *slavery*, not its mere *incidents* that I hated."[37] Uncertainty, combined with powerlessness under the arbitrary, changing will or moods of one's current owner, these constituted for him the "overshadowing evil" of slavery.

When in the course of this book it was denied that the dramatic, episodic infliction of pain is all there is to cruelty, it was *not* meant that the slave's life was *happy*. What was meant was that the "terrible crushing and grinding" involves more than a dramatic moment of pain, and sometimes involves no dramatic moments at all. It is a condition, a situation that has a history, that lasts from dawn to night, and into the night, throughout the waking hours, and even into the dreams of its victims. And this uncertainty had to do not only with the day-to-day moods of one's master (or later of the local white population), but also with one's own future—whether one would be sold down the river because of economic need or because of a whim or because of the death of one's owner, etc. It also had to do with one's past, which was systematically stripped from all slaves' memories.

To know is not always enough; it may give one power, but by itself it does not always give one enough power. A slave's knowledge that he will be lynched if he strikes a white man could be of some help to him. But the knowledge did not free him from slavery. Powerlessness under an inimical will *and* uncertainty *together* constitute the "terrible crushing and grinding," the "overshadowing evil."

There is another aspect of the cruel situation which still, though attenuated, obtains in the United States, both North and South. At the beginning of Ralph Ellison's *Invisible Man*, the narrator says:

> I am invisible, understand, simply because people refuse to see me. Like the bodiless heads you see sometimes in circus sideshows, it is as though I have been surrounded by mirrors of hard, distorting glass. When they approach me they see only my surroundings, themselves, or figments of their imagination—indeed, everything and anything except me.[38]

He goes on to say that the invisibility of "a man of substance, of flesh and bone, fiber and liquids" is not simply physical; it has to do with

...the construction of their *inner* eyes, those eyes with which they look through their physical eyes upon reality.[39]

This metaphor is connected with W.E.B. Du Bois's description of the black man as "shut out from their world by a vast veil."[40] But its point is that men—black or white—do not see individuals or even human beings when they see a black man—they see "figments of their imagination." In the days of Frederick Douglass a black man was presumed a slave if he carried no evidence of his freedom. At one point in his autobiographical narrative he—as a matter of course—describes a conversation between himself and a train conductor in which the conductor in a kindly way asks him, "But you have something to show that you are a free man, have you not?"[41]

That same presumption took different forms after the Emancipation Proclamation, but it was still the presumption that the black man was by virtue of being black the groceries of the white man, the product and instrument of the white man's will, a passive being there for the white man's use—until proved otherwise. This presumption of passivity made it possible for the white man to make of the Negro what he wished to make of him—out of figments of his own imagination, and out of a few scattered, squalid facts that the white man himself had brought into being by the institution of slavery.

Thus was born Sambo, the eternal child, the eternal dependent, happy, though given to unaccountable moods of depression, lazy, enjoying the banjo and the dance, passionately religious, but passive in most other things—a rather spirited but lazy, overgrown child. This was the image laid upon the dark skin of the black people by those who had the power to do it.

In Jerzy Kosinski's *The Painted Bird* there is a man named Lekh, who keeps birds. When his stupid sex partner Ludmila does not turn up for a while he becomes silently enraged, stares at the birds in their cages, chooses the strongest one, ties it to his wrist, and prepares "striking paints of different colors which he mixed together from the most varied components." When he gets the right color he paints the bird's "wings, head, and breast in rainbow hues until it became more dappled and vivid than a bouquet of wildflowers." Then he takes the painted bird into a thick forest, and holds him until he attracts birds of the same species. When enough birds are flying close by, he releases the prisoner, who first soars, happy and free, and then comes down to his flock. First the birds are confused, while the painted bird tries to enter the flock, tries to convince them that despite its new colors it is one of them. But one by one the other birds peel off from the flock and attack him, and he eventually drops to the ground, where Lekh closely examines the effect of their beaks while the blood seeps through its colored feathers.

For centuries now men have been painting members of their own species with abstractions "mixed together from the most varied components." One of them was Sambo, who wanted only to serve, needed protection, and could sing like a bird. *For his own good* you kept him in slavery (as well as for the economic and social good of the planters). And if he tried to rejoin the species, why it was only to keep him from being "uppity," to teach him his "place" that one used the whips, the dogs, the mobs, the white man's slave laws, and later the Jim Crow laws and restrictive covenants in housing. After all, Sambo was *really* a man who could not endure freedom of body and of conscience. Despite any appearances to the contrary he was *really* a perpetually dependent, *really* a happy child. Paint the bird with your own garish colors and society will do the rest. Call him "racially inferior," or "childlike," and no matter what he does to show his own true colors will be in vain: people will get used to excluding him from the species, and they will get used to attacking him when he tries to get back into the species.

What such abstractions as "nigger" do is much the same thing that all abstractions do: they eliminate individual differences, differences between individual cases. They help us (or lead us) to treat a given entity *generically*, as if its individual markings and powers are irrelevant to the problem at hand. Healthy abstractions—abstractions that can be revised or refuted by particular facts—can guide us in our treatment of individual cases. But rigid abstractions cannot be revised or refuted by particular facts. They look as if they discuss individuals, but they are actually devices for disregarding the individual. Such a device is embodied in the following phrase: "He appears to be intelligent and hard-working, but *they're all alike, deep down* he's *just* a lazy nigger." These rigid abstractions are what the Southerner "understands" when he says that he "understands niggers." Such an understanding is the most potent instrument of cruelty, because the powerlessness of the individual victim to assert *himself* and make a difference is central to cruelty. Rigid abstractions may be useful for helping us to destroy chickens (and not leading us to think about this particular chicken, its life and death); and they can also help us to use and destroy our fellow human beings. During the Nazi Regime, expressions like "Final Solution" and "Jewish Question" combined with statistics to keep the level of abstraction so high that Germans became convinced they were not killing individual persons.[42]

Such rigid abstractions help us to endure the paradox of cruelty: in killing a nigger you are doing something abstractly justifiable; in fact, you *seem* to be doing something abstract, not concrete or actual. It is when, despite their rigidity, you descend from such abstractions that you begin to see the unjustifiability of that particular act of destruction.

But men seldom make such a descent on their own initiative; their abstractions, especially when they are enforced by a dominant community around them, become easy to inhabit, as well as profitable. It is the *victim*, who is and feels his own individuality, his own power to move his own body and to have his own thoughts, who does not find them easy and profitable. From his point of view cruelty is unjustifiable—that is, unjustifiable until he begins himself to use these abstractions when he thinks about himself. When he joins the victimizer in using them he is co-operating in the act of cruelty.

In the midst of all the criticisms that the aristocracy of medieval Europe drew down upon itself from the urban bourgeoisie, the papacy, the peasants, and the monarchy itself, the lord of a castle was admired and imitated. Even the peasantry, who were unarmed for the most part, and directly under the power of the lord of the castle, long remained loyal to their lords by that combination of *amor et timor*, love and fear, that often is felt by the inferior towards the superior.

In the case of American slavery with its castles and its peculiar power imbalance, this *amor et timor* took a rather complicated form. Aside from the uncertainties regarding his immediate and distant future, the black was spiritually immobilized by the paint the white man laid upon him. His situation of powerlessness, his uncertainties about his own tribal or familial past, and his uncertainties about his future combined to make *him* think of *himself* as a nigger or an inferior in all ways. With the language of the whites the black slaves, emerging from their "seasoning" after the Middle Passage from Africa, received words like "nigger," and the whole dreadful wealth of associations that the word "black" carries in predominantly white countries. Not only is there blackmail, a black market, a black heart, but in the Bible as well as in much of the theology and literature of the West, the connotations of the word "black" are often negative: in the fifth verse of the first chapter of The Song of Solomon we read, "I am black but comely, o ye daughters of Jerusalem." And even Frederick Douglass, that committed defender of black pride, found himself saying that the black man in America was

> maltreated with impunity by anyone, no matter how black his heart, so he has a white skin.[43]

Even *he* found himself describing a vicious man as "black-hearted."

The paint on the painted bird seeped down to his soul, and with it the despisal that was mixed in the paint, despisal that sees no individuals, only an inferior. And seeing himself with the same *"inner* eyes" as the whites, he began to despise himself, to think of himself as something less or other than human, what Ellison called "a phantom in other people's minds." In an effort to escape his blackness, with all that it connotes in a white society, he straightened his hair, tried to bleach out his complexion, even sharpened his nose, tried to become what William H. Ferris in *The African Abroad* described as "a black white man," tried to become a "Negro-Saxon."[44] In both the North and the South, shades of lightness affected one's status in the Negro community, and one found oneself in a society of one's own degree of lightness, while yearning for a "higher society" lighter (though still black) than one's own. And so, for instance, the "Brown Fellowship" of light-skinned blacks was founded in Charleston, South Carolina in 1790 as an aristocracy in a hierarchy the top of which was the White Man and the bottom of which was the pure African Black Man.

This is no place to summarize what various books have shown about the *fascinosum* the Black man felt for his victimizer. E. Franklin Frazier has attacked the issue of white-worship boldly in *Negro Youth at the Crossways,* and Wallace Thurman has done it in *The Blacker the Berry,* a novel that treats of the hatred of blackness on the part of many black people.

And all of this was not simply another example of weakness in awe of strength. The *policy* of the white slave-owner was to see to it, as Frederick Douglass puts it, that black people were

> Trained from the cradle up to think and feel that their masters were superiors, and invested with a sort of sacredness . . . [45]

And Douglass goes on to point out that "there were few who could rise above the control which that sentiment exercised."

The "Christian" churches of America contributed to this useful sentiment of white sacredness. Isolated as they were, being mostly Protestant, churches were in the hands of the local white populations, and these groups wanted the churches to purvey such wisdom as "Servant, obey thy masters" and that aristocratically condescending accolade for the utterly subservient: "Well done, thou good and faithful servant." In Catholic countries like Brazil, where the Church was centralized, all men were *defined* as ensouled beings, capable of salvation; and so there was frequently a different way of educating the slaves, a way that did not always make the white man alone sacred.[46] But with no centrally expressed and administered ecclesiastical authority and no broadly humane theology—except the emphasis on the sinfulness of man—with a theology tailored to the local needs of the slave-owners and other whites, the white man could use religion as a way of investing his "own limitless power" with divinity.[47]

The process of making God the author of slavery and the white man God's lily-white deputy, while the black man was a hard-handed, dark-colored target of God's displeasure, this process Douglass called "slaveholding priestcraft." Such priestcraft combined with the totally imbalanced power situation between white and blacks helped to accomplish the final passivity of the black man.

There are various psychological theories that try to explicate the mechanisms of the slaveholding priestcraft and its effects on black people long after 1863. For instance, the Freudians, notably Anna Freud in *The Ego and the Mechanisms of Defense*, speak of identification with the aggressor as a defense against his great power; victims try to lose themselves in the omnipotent enemy and this "childish dependence" on the omnipotent "big daddy" is described by the Freudians as "the final stage of passive adaptation" and "survival through surrender." In a previous chapter we used the broad theological metaphor of the *fascinosum;* and we saw it operating in the Gothic Tale. The Freudians have discussed it as a mechanism of defense, a way of surviving under absolute power.[48]

Harry Stack Sullivan with his doctrine of the "significant others," the compact majority with more or less absolute authority, has another theory, one that emphasizes the environment of the victim of absolute power more than it emphasizes the mechanism within the victim. A situation in which the weaker member cannot select his own "significant others," his own authorities, is called by Sullivan a "closed system"—what we have been using the metaphor of the castle to describe. In a closed system the weak member has "no lines to the outside in any matter . . . " and finds himself embodying his highest ideals in the significant others who have trapped him.[49] His appraisals of himself become the "reflected appraisals" the powerful others have made of him.

Still another interpersonal theory of victimization occurs in "role psychology." This theory has been combined with Sullivan's "significant others" theory by H. H. Gerth and C. Wright Mills, and it describes the way the impotent live under the powerful by accepting the god-like power of assigning their roles, their patterns of appropriate behavior. Theodore R. Sarbin, in a paper entitled "The Culture of Poverty," shows how a participant in the culture of poverty becomes a non-person by having a way of life rigidly imposed upon him by his place in the social situation.[50] He is assigned a role that has very little freedom of choice, a role that takes all his time and energy to "perform," and one for which he is not *esteemed* when he is successful. This is the man Sarbin describes as "degraded," the man who in the twentieth century is usually geographically isolated in a ghetto and who shares with the slave the sense that all his functions in society are dictated from "above" laid down by those happy ones who hold the power and the prestige of Olympian deities.

As we have often noticed, our task in this book is not to penetrate the depths and the exact mechanisms of human victimization. I have mentioned these theories only to show that the *fascinosum* felt by the isolated victim of great power is not simply a theological or novelistic concern—it is the concern of many social scientists who seek to penetrate the manner in which men come to revere or at least live patiently under an immensely powerful "other." This accommodation to the compact majority is one of the main instruments the victimizer finds at his fingertips when his power is—or can be—great enough. By means of it the victim feels that he is in *some* way identified with what Otto called the "wholly other" the *mysterium* that holds so much power. Just as the music that preceded Melmoth's cruel proposals soothed the fears of his victims, so the sense of fascination with the all-powerful helped sooth the anxieties of many slaves and helped enthrall "free" black people degraded by prejudice and poverty.

We have not come to the end of our account of how the black people of America were made passive recipients of an inferior "role" assigned by the whites. There is one more step to take, one hinted at toward the beginning of the previous section. The identification of whiteness with moral superiority, beauty, and goodness, could not, of course, be complete. The black people were still black, and the white people took every opportunity to remind them of this. They could for a while "identify with the aggressor" or in the language of Harry Stack Sullivan "internalize" the standards laid down by the "significant others," but they could do this only for a while and only with a part of their consciousness: for they were black, and that black was different from white was the task of the whole social structure to keep before their minds.

Now this is not to say that they simply despised themselves in their identification with the significant others. If they despised themselves single-mindedly this in itself could have given them the elaborate masochistic pleasure Theodore Reik so carefully describes in his *Masochism In Modern Man*. They could have become full-time masochists with the special pleasures of "victory through defeat" that masochists enjoy.

But masochism was not the way the black people "internalized" or "identified" with the power structure. The American Negro managed to love the obvious joys of life too much to indulge in the fanciful, cerebral game of masochism. And so he both loved his life *and* despised it, sometimes at the same time, eating the food he liked, telling the stories he liked, singing the songs he liked, dancing the dances he liked. And this was the ultimate cruelty visited upon the black man—a soul torn in two different directions.

No man has expressed this tearing more memorably than has W.E.B. Du Bois in *The Souls of Black Folks*. Here is an often quoted passage:

> After the Egyptian and Indian, the Greek and Roman, the Teuton and Mongolian, the Negro is a sort of seventh son, born with a veil, and gifted with second-sight in this American world— a world which yields him no true self-consciousness, but only lets him see himself through the revelation of the other world. It is a peculiar sensation, this double-consciousness, this sense of always looking at one's self through the eyes of others, of measuring one's soul by the tape of a world that looks on in amused contempt and pity. One ever feels his two-ness,—an American, a Negro; two souls, two thoughts, two unreconciled strivings; two warring ideals in one dark body, whose dogged strength alone keeps it from being torn asunder.[51]

Lift a cup with that black hand, and you find yourself asking: Is that the way it's *supposed* to be done? And wouldn't it be better if that were a white hand? And yet it is my hand, and it is black. Again Du Bois:

> He would not bleach his Negro soul in a flood of white Americanism, for he knows that Negro blood has a message for the world.[52]

At least when he is most strong he would not do this, would not try to do the utterly impossible—but then he is not always strong enough to avoid this fascination with the whiteness of the lily-white.

There is another, quite different way of putting this ultimate cruelty, this ultimate crushing and grinding. Gunnar Myrdal wrote in the forties a book entitled *An American Dilemma*. The argument of this massive work is that the American creed of liberty and equality for all is flatly contradicted by the white Americans' treatment of black Americans. He points out that the Jeffersonian ideal of equals in a free society is and always has been violated by our practice with regard to our black citizens—violated in every way one can violate a pious intention—psychologically, sociologically, economically, politically, theologically. Violated in every way a man can violate a man. He shows in all of these dimensions how this violation took place because the powerful victimizer was able to isolate his victim and overpower him in plantations and ghettoes across the nation in what we have been calling "castles."[53]

Myrdal's book analyzes in social terms what we have been calling the paradox of cruelty.[54] White America found the inferiority of the black people *both* unjustifiable in theory and justifiable in fact. And as we have been seeing in this chapter, that same ambivalence appeared in the minds of Negroes in their attitudes toward themselves. Myrdal's book shows how firmly Americans believe in liberty and equality while they with equal firmness believe in keeping the black man in an inferior place in our society.

The one trouble with this classic work lies in terms like "dilemma" and "contradiction." These are logical terms—not psychological or *totalistic*. People can live with dilemmas and contradictions *if they are the perpetrators of them* and are seeing them in such objective terms. Charles Silberman puts it exactly in *Crisis in Black and White:*

> The tragedy of race relations in the United States is that there is no American Dilemma. White Americans are not torn and tortured by the conflict between their devotion to the American creed and their actual behavior. They are upset by the current state of race relations, to be sure. But what troubles them is not that justice is being denied but that their peace is being shattered and their business interrupted.[55]

The American torture is in the flesh, blood, bone, and mind of the *victim* of it—the Black man. It is not simply a dilemma or a contradiction, or a riot or an injustice—it is the paralyzing horror, the ultimate uncertainty about what America is and about what *I am* that is the issue. The most intimate cruelty of all is not to know what America is, and not to know who one is here. Remember Du Bois's words: "two souls, two thoughts, two unreconciled strivings; two warring ideals in one dark body, whose dogged strength alone keeps it from being torn asunder." This is the ultimate cruelty of being a black American living in the psychological, economic, and political shadow of slavery. It is by tearing himself asunder that the black man completes the white man's cruelty and becomes an embodiment of the paradox of cruelty.

Throughout this book the imagination has been one of our main topics. Of course "the imagination" is as deceptive an abstraction as "the beautiful" or "the good," because it means so many things in so many different circumstances. For instance, for Sade it was a source of capricious disorder; and for Kant and Coleridge it was a way of ordering and understanding the world. If we take man's imagination to be his ability to construct and comprehend "pictures" that never were in actuality (or in history) exactly the same as the picture, then we can talk broadly about this remarkable tendency in man. Either the pictures can be plainly visible to the physical eye—like the engravings of Hogarth—or they can be pictures available to Ellison's "inner eye." Of course, all the pictures we have been discussing involve not only spatial images, but words, and very abstract words at that—"cruelty" is such a word, and so is "victim"; certainly "destruction" is, and so are most of the key terms of this book. And so the differences between Hogarth's "pictur'd morals" and Sade's "dissertations" on cruelty that help his strong beings catch their breath while continuing their pleasures between "demonstrations," all of these styles of moralizing differ from each other only in degree. Some people's imaginations emphasize concrete spatial images more than they do ideas or words that have to be laid out in temporal or logical sequence; others emphasize such ideas or words more than they do spatial pictures. But the main point, the main "family resemblance" (as Ludwig Wittgenstein would put it) amongst imaginings is that they supplement or round out or complete our everyday perceptions of things and people. Imagination is what people do to the facts to make them whole, complete. Of course, as Kant and Coleridge pointed out, this "doing" happens quietly, even unconsciously to us while we are looking at "the facts," so that man, with his active imagination, probably never faces facts naked and bare, as they "really" are.

But with such problematic speculations we are not concerned. All the imaginings we have studied are efforts men have made to round out their fragmentary experience, to give it an understandable shape. Hogarth's completion of experience was primarily laid out in spatial images, and these images showed the power of the victim to bring about a terminal cruelty on the head of his victimizer. Sade's completion of experience drew images for that "inner eye" by making us imitate in our own minds the destructive erotic power of the strong one and the hopeless passive weakness of his victim. The horror tale celebrated a victimizer vaster and more powerful than even Sade's, but it also gave the victim powerful allies, and gave the victim herself often endless powers to resist the villain. Think only of *Melmoth the Wanderer* and of his failure to break even *one* will, with all his powers.

But when we leave art and enter history, when we see, for instance, the operations of cruelty in the history of the black people in America, we find ourselves dealing not with the imaginations of artists or other spectators of cruelty; we find ourselves dealing with the imagination of the *participants* in the cruel relationship. Hogarth, Sade, Walpole, Maturin, Lewis, all exhibited their own efforts to round out and comprehend the cruelties people visit on each other. But the white man's Sambo, his painted bird, and the black man's accommodation to that paint, the white man's usage of the spatial metaphor of "inferiority" (and its assorted metaphors like "nigger" and "coon") helped create and perpetuate the cruel relationship. And so did the actions the white man performed in the process of "seeing" the black man as a passive creature, like a mule, or like a bag of groceries. These actions, combined with the black man's actions under his *own* images of his own inferiority, these images all helped to perpetuate in those closed systems the cruel relationship. The white man's imagination kept him in the ascendancy; the black man's imagination, pushed not only by the image-laden actions of the whites, but by the power of the whites, kept him passive, kept him in the cruel relationship.

And so now we are dealing with the imaginations of participants in this relationship. But of course it is silly to forget all those worldly forces that contributed to and supported the imaginations of the victims and the victimizers, the economic and political forces. All we are noticing here is that imagination helped complete, round out the effects of these forces on men's minds and bodies. During the reign of King Cotton in the deep South, the economic necessity for cheap reliable labor and the physical as well as political possibility of obtaining and holding this kind of labor, these and other hard forces created the basic stuff from which the imagination of man arises, like a castle built of the same sort of stone as that which supports and surrounds it.

Before taking the next step in our exploration, it is important to see that the way the imagination rounds out facts is not with little painted pictures that are purely spatial—either to the physical or to the inner eye. It rounds out the facts by generating actions and passions, by producing words and judgments, by making us live in certain ways, with certain styles. Imagination is not a peep show with pictures that we passively stare at; it is a way of acting and feeling and thinking. *If* there are little images the planter "sees" in his mind when he thinks of or sees a black man in the flesh, those little images themselves are of little importance—it is his whole way of thinking and feeling and acting with regard to that black man working in his cotton field that is his way of comprehending that black man. And it is all this, not simply the little images that may or may not "exist" in his mind, that is what we are calling his "imagination." His images are not as important to us as what he *does* to define them. The word "Sambo" and the image of a black man grinning and eating a ripe red watermelon crouched down in a field—these are only a small part of the imagination we have been speaking of; the comprehensive way that the planter judges and treats the flesh and blood black men he encounters, this constitutes his full-blown imagination regarding Negroes.

On the other hand, the comprehensive way the black man thinks of the white man and of himself when he tries to bleach his skin or straighten his hair or even "pass" in white society, these are *his* imagination, his way of facing that planter or that compact majority wielding such terrible power over his life.

But there is one element of the black man's imagination—and of the white man's for that matter—that we have not mentioned in this book. That one element is of such importance that to leave it out is at once to fail to see in its fullness the history of the black people in America and to fail to see the main point about cruelty that this book is trying to make.

Ever since the first black man jumped into the sea during the Middle Passage or would not eat or died of misery in the hold, this element that we have been neglecting was appearing in the imaginations and lives of black men. It is the element—so difficult to name, because it, like the term "the imagination" takes so many forms—that *refuses passivity under another man or group of men.* This refusal is an action only fleetingly dreamt of by Sade and by all those who condone the cruel relationship. This refusal is the "water" on the "fire" that Sade talks about, *the* obstacle to the joys of the dungeon or the locked apartment bedroom. And this refusal on the part of the black people of America has been their main hope, though it was, and perhaps to a degree still is, small indeed, as small as the imagination is when it is not adequately supported by economic and political facts.

Still, *that* it is their main hope and *how* it constitutes that hope are very important to us. Once we see these things we shall have before us a rounded out picture of cruelty, as well as some hints toward a way of understanding race relations in America.

Now the refusal to accept all commands, the refusal to be groceries, can itself be put in picturesque ways: we can see it as the refusal on the part of the bird to let the paint sink into his flesh; or we can see it as the refusal of the victim to be fascinated, "enthralled" (again, that vitally ambiguous word) by the vast power of the victimizer. We can see it as "raw" courage—the courage of Ernest Thompson Seton's Pacing Mustang, who when he was at last roped

> . . . defied the swinging, slashing rope and the gunshot fired in air, in vain attempt to turn his frenzied course. Up, up and on, above the sheerest cliff he dashed and sprang away into the vacant air, down—down—two hundred downward feet to fall, and land upon the rocks below, a lifeless wreck—but free.[56]

There were slave revolts (far more frequent than most students know). There were ambiguous but deeply protesting slave songs. There were individual actions (protecting a black woman or striking back at a white man). There were many organizations, both clandestine and nationally known, that physically removed men from the cruel relationship. Some of these removed him illegally, as did the Underground Railroad, and others protected him legally, as did the National Association for the Advancement of Colored People. There were other organizations that sometimes tried to remove the black people from the shadow of slavery educationally, as did the great Negro universities like Fisk and Howard. Still others tried to remove the black people from it spiritually as did the Southern Christian Leadership Conference under Martin Luther King, Jr. And there are many more *actions* that are expressions of a new image of the black man. They are part of his body and soul; they inform his life, they are the "obstacle" to the cruel relationship that Sade so much feared, and that he tried so hard to imagine away. Though they often issued in violently as well as quietly cruel events even bloodier than the ones they were trying to punish and prevent, they managed slowly over the centuries in both the black man's and the white man's mind to crack the patterns of images we have been describing in this chapter.

Of course there are many differences between ways of standing up, ways of cracking the images and changing the power situation. For instance, some ways were more rebellious, even more destructive, than others. In W.E.B. Du Bois's essay "On Mr. Booker T. Washington and Others" there is a brief summary of such differences. Du Bois says that there are three ways of reacting to the relationships between whites and blacks. One way was by "adjustment and submission" to the white man's belief in the inferiority of the Negro.[57] This way, Du Bois goes on, Booker T. Washington was following in his famous Atlanta Compromise Speech of 1895 when instead of asking for the vote or for higher education he asked the Negro to "Cast down your bucket where you are" and "learn to dignify and glorify common labor" while educating himself only to be "patient, faithful, law-abiding, and unresentful . . . ." Du Bois was convinced that this kind of approach, this "silent submission to civic inferiority" is "bound to sap the manhood of any race in the long run."

Another approach is that

> . . . spiritually descended from Toussaint the Savior, through Gabriel, Vesey, and Turner, and they represent the attitude of revolt and revenge; they hate the white South blindly and distrust the white race generally.[58]

Du Bois believed that this approach is shared by those advocating emigration from the United States. But this was not his way — Du Bois's way was more regardful of individual differences amongst Negroes than was Washington's and less hopeful about violent or sudden solutions than the advocates of revolt or emigration. He wanted black people to have the right to vote, civic equality (in all of its many forms), and education according to the individual's ability. He wanted the black people to be able to live according to the American Declaration of Independence:

> We hold these truths to be self-evident: That all men are created equal; that they are endowed by their Creator with certain unalienable rights; that among these are life, liberty, and the pursuit of happiness.[59]

Moreover, he believed that this way of life for the black people of America was *possible*, if appropriate measures were taken.

It is not the purpose of this book to explore these ways—let alone to decide which way will be the most effective. Still, it seems plain to me that the way of Booker T. Washington's Atlanta Compromise Speech of 1895 is too close to slavery to be a protest—and I use the phrase "close to" both chronologically and philosophically. Washington was very conscious of the recent "leap from slavery to freedom" (as he called it in that speech). Because of his and his people's proximity to that "leap," he felt that "It is at the bottom of life we must begin, and not at the top." Such an attitude, at least for the sixties in the twentieth century, seems less like protest than like submission—and it seemed to be this even in Du Bois's time, which was only a few years after the speech.

But pursuing such issues will take us away from the main task of this book: to clarify our understanding of cruelty. At this point in our task we are trying to see only that men can "stand up" in various ways to cruelty, and that this standing up is a refusal to remain passive.

To exhibit a large, overarching pattern of this refusal to be passive let us go back to the image of a machine and of the grain of sand that people can put into it to interrupt its smooth action. Yankel Meisel was not a perfect example of refusal to accommodate the cruel relationship—he was not rebelling; he simply failed to sew on some buttons, and he screamed too loudly when he was being beaten to death. These are not full-scale refusals like the ones that occur almost everywhere in the history of the black people in America.

In seeking out a pattern of resistance, we shall use both the machine-image and the image of a castle or isolated place where the strength of the victimizer is maximized. Imagine Poe's machine in "The Pit and the Pendulum." It consists of a pendulum with its razor edge coming closer and closer to the victim, and is functioning inside a dungeon in Toledo, Spain, at the time of the Inquisition. The machine threatens him, but so does the dungeon in its own way. The story has some interesting resemblances to our over-all image of cruelty. For instance, at a point of great despair, the victim, tied underneath a slowly descending, razor-edged pendulum gazes at it with horror, and then he

> ...struggled to force myself upward against the sweep of the fearful scimitar. And then I fell suddenly calm, and lay smiling at the glittering death, as a child at some rare bauble.[60]

The victim is never perfectly passive—he can at least seek to hasten his death or he can act by being fascinated by the glittering power of his destroyer.

And the story in other ways exhibits the main imagery we have been using. When the victim is freed from his bonds by the rats chewing the food he rubbed into these cloth bonds, Poe writes:

> ...I slid from the embrace of the bandage and beyond the reach of the scimitar. For the moment, at least, *I was free.*
>
> Free!—and in the grasp of the Inquisition!...My every motion was undoubtedly watched. Free!—I had but escaped death in one form of agony, to be delivered unto worse than death in some other.[61]

In short, he was still in the dungeon, just as the black man was still in various castles after the Emancipation Proclamation of 1863.

And there is still another similarity between the history of the black people and this little story. The similarity lies in the final escape of the victim: at the end of the story, outsiders break into the dungeon and release him:

> An outstretched arm caught my own as I fell fainting into the abyss. It was that of General Lasalle. The French army had entered Toledo. The Inquisition was in the hands of its enemies.[62]

This too is part of the pattern we are exploring—the victim is helped by allies; he needs that help; otherwise the victimizer is too strong.

But let us turn again to history in order to see cruelty writ large. Arthur I. Waskow, in a useful book entitled *From Race Riot to Sit-In*,[63] tells us about a series of events that occurred in a machine-castle situation, and he also tells us about a grain of sand, and a breach in a castle wall.

The scene is the little Negro country church at Hoop Spur, in east central Arkansas, and the time is September 30, 1919, a year in which race riots were occurring in various places in the United States. According to the white account, some deputy sheriffs, on business unrelated to what actually happened, were passing the little church and had to stop near it because of a punctured tire. According to that same account, Negro guards fired on these innocent white men and then launched an attack on the whole white party. The reason the Negroes did this was that they were afraid whites would discover the Negroes' plans to rise up and massacre whites all across Phillips County, Arkansas.

According to the black account, the people inside that little church were not planning to massacre whites; they were holding a meeting of their branch of the "Progressive Farmers and Household Union of America," a group of Negro Phillips County share-croppers and tenant farmers who objected to the small amount of money they were getting for their cotton and the large amount of money they had to pay for their supplies. The target of their objections was the plantation owners, who sold their cotton for them and sold them their supplies. A branch of the Progressive Union was meeting in that little church, planning to demand accurate accounting from the planters, when they were interrupted by shots fired from the outside into the church. And the black account goes on: it was only after these shots were fired that the Negroes left the church and attacked the whites. The next day, October 1, the whites burned down the church in order to destroy the evidence of their having fired into the church and initiated the bloodshed.

Waskow sums up the evidence with a judgment in favor of the Negroes' version,[64] but our task here is not to re-decide this case. It is to describe its main outlines as part of our explanation of cruelty. Whoever called forth the bloodshed that occurred at Hoop Spur, the fact is plain that it interrupted a meeting of the Progressive Union in which the planters' obviously exploitative prices were under attack. Plans were being made by the victims to correct them. As Waskow puts it

> What remained constant in the changing Arkansas story, . . . was that Negro sharecroppers had determined, like their big-city brethren, to "fight back."[65]

Both the stated aims of the Progressive Union and the killing by the Negroes of some whites make *this* clear.

What we shall be looking for in this one example, the Arkansas riots of 1919, is a pattern of resistance, a way the grain of sand gets dropped into the machine of institutional cruelty. Surely the economic exploitation of the Negro sharecroppers by the planters is as much a shadow of slavery, a machine of slavery, an intimate way of maiming men's ways of life, as slavery itself or Jim Crow. Poverty carefully enforced along color lines maims the minds and bodies of all its victims.

We shall find that the grain of sand in the machine, the light in the shadow, the resistance to the unfettered power of the white majority follows a certain pattern. Either that resistance stays local and is crushed or it expands and breaks down the machine. Abolitionism expanded into the life and thought of Northerners, and when Abraham Lincoln was elected to the Presidency, resistance to "the peculiar institution" expanded further because of Lincoln's desire to save the Union. Resistance took the form of an industrialized North invading a predominantly agricultural South, and the machine was broken (though, as we have seen, the dungeon was not destroyed).

And this is important for us to see because cruelty cannot be writ large unless resistance to it is also writ large. In physics "work" is defined as the overcoming of resistance; open-textured words like "cruelty" cannot be so readily defined; the resistance that helps define them is not to be measured precisely. But the meaning of "cruelty" can be most clearly understood not by reading Sade's novels wherein non-entities writhe gracefully and die, or by observing or participating in machines where the weak are efficiently ground very small. It is to be understood in relation to the resistance it calls forth, in relation to the actions that crystallize the otherwise quiet desperation of the weak.

You can understand a force like cruelty best by seeing the nature and force of what can *stop* it. When the weak get strong enough they show the amount of power that has been exerted on them; in their outrage, in their hate and in their fear they show just how destructive the cruelty they have experienced has been. When you see a mouse strike out from its corner at the great cat who is torturing it, you begin to understand what torture is to a victim, that it can produce such extraordinary effects, such passionate action. If you ignore that passionate reaction you are in danger of ignoring the destructiveness of cruelty. Children watching a cinema do not understand the killing of a villain, or a hero, unless they see some retaliatory hatred or resistance. Cruelty without that passionate resistance can look simply like smashing a potato chip.

And so let us consider further the pattern of resistance followed by the Progressive Union of Negro Sharecroppers who shot at those white citizens. After the interchange of shots, during which both Negroes and whites were killed, hundreds of Negroes were arrested and brought to Helena, Arkansas for interrogation. While this was happening, many whites took it upon themselves to find more Negroes participating in the Progressive Union. On October 1 some of these men reached Ratio, Arkansas, where a certain lawyer named U.S. Bratton (who had shown much courage and skill in defending Negroes from being subjected to peonage) was advising Negroes of that area how to "fight back" at a certain big-plantation owner. These Negroes made up another branch of the Progressive Union. Bratton was arrested and taken to Elaine (the area in which the Hoop Spur incident had occurred) where he was threatened with lynching, and had to be chained in the back of a store and defended by a deputy sheriff. He was the key man threatening to open the gates to the Phillips County castle and let the world in or let the world look in.

In a few days, the white feeling against Bratton had cooled, but by that time five whites had been killed and approximately sixty black persons were killed.[66] In the course of all this not a single white man was arrested, except one who was then considered to be on the side of the Negroes. This is a crucial point: the white majority, excited by the plantation owners and their creatures and supported by the poor-white mobs, had trapped the blacks in Phillips County, Arkansas, and were using the legal machinery of that county (as well as of the state of Arkansas) to smash the Negroes' "rebellion." In the course of the investigation on the part of the state, county, and municipal governments, Negroes were tortured (by electric shocks and mock hanging) into confessing to perpetrating an armed insurrection against the whites.[67] Later, in 1921, two of the whites involved in these investigations gave elaborate accounts of the brutality used in extorting confessions.

The whole case against the blacks who still survived was put into the hands of a so-called "Committee of Seven," made up of white Arkansas businessmen and local white law-enforcement officers. One of the white businessmen, E.M. Allen, had a 21,000 acre cotton plantation near Elaine, with 750 sharecroppers on the plantation. This man was chairman of the Committee empowered to supervise the prosecution of the black persons under indictment.

With the help of the Seven a grand jury met for three days to hear testimony, and on one day, October 30, indicted seventy-three Negroes. Attorneys for the Negroes were appointed by the local court from the local bar, with no questioning of the Negroes as to their preference. None of the lawyers challenged a candidate for the all-white juries; none asked for time to prepare a defense; none had talked with the defendants; none questioned the confessions of insurrection or the evidence later shown to have been gotten by torture. The first six men produced no defense witnesses and did not themselves take the stand. In brief, after trials ranging from an hour to two or three hours, and after jury-consultations of four to ten minutes for each case, twelve black men were convicted of first degree murder and were sentenced to death.

There were no lynchings; with respectability and legality

the state of Arkansas showed, as Waskow puts it "how effective sheer physical force could be operated with legal sanction . . . "[68] It was all very speedy, very peaceful, very law-abiding. And twelve men were swiftly condemned to death.

At this point in his account of the Arkansas riot, A.I. Waskow inserts an interesting paragraph:

> But even legal suppression could not restore to Arkansas the apathetic and the hopeless Negro that had been its mudsill for a generation. In December, a "white moderate" recoiled with horror at the militance still expressed by Negroes in the state. "I spoke at a Negro conference last Sunday night at Hot Springs," he reported. "The negro who spoke before me had much to say about freedom and the crowd was deeply stirred. I spoke of duty and Christian discipleship and got no response." . . . The fighting-back spirit had not died, although the fighting itself was over.[69]

Other groups, including the now vigorous offshoot of the Niagara Movement, the National Association for the Advancement of Colored People, condemned the trials, and there were mass meetings in New York and Philadelphia to proclaim the injustice of the trials.

But the central point lies in that paragraph of Waskow's: the Negroes were no longer passive; they were active, if only re-active to white cruelty. And the empty words like "duty" and "Christian discipleship" were obviously lies to them. They felt what Myrdal called the "American Dilemma," and they reacted to their awareness of this pious hypocrisy.

From that spirit of fighting back, but also from the support of groups and individuals with bases outside the castle-machine of Phillips County, the Arkansas case became a force that kept alive the issue in the minds of many men. Articles appeared in national media stating the arguments for the Negroes, and a four-year campaign was launched to protect those convicted.

In the course of those four years America learned of the slavish labor that the plantation owners were exacting from those Negroes in Phillips County, and the trials brought financial, intellectual, and political pressures to bear upon the state of Arkansas. In the course of those trials, again in the language of Waskow,

... the federal government demonstrated that ... its second and third thoughts constrained it to a degree of impartiality unknown to the local authorities.[70]

The federal government had at first left the castle-machine of Arkansas intact; but in the end, despite the fact that every commercial and political organization in Phillips County opposed clemency to the convicted Negroes, the current president of the NAACP pleaded the case before the Supreme Court of the United States. As Justice Holmes put it, it was then seen that "counsel, jury and judge were swept to the fatal end by an irresistible wave of public passion, and that the State Courts failed to correct the wrong . . . ."[71]

The Court saw the injustices but finally recommended that the state courts be the arena in which the final battles in favor of these convicted men would be fought. In April of 1923 six of the defendants were freed on a technicality. After nine years, all the remaining death sentences were commuted to twelve years in prison terms. As Waskow summarizes the case, "the world outside Arkansas was too powerful an opponent and too attractive a lure to resist."[72] National opinion, national power (especially on the part of the NAACP and its remarkable leaders) overwhelmed the Arkansas solution to the killings that happened on and after September 20, 1919.

It is important to notice that all through those four years the state of Arkansas had as its main justification for its treatment of the Negroes its desire to keep the foundations of society orderly and respectable. The main argument, from the beginning to the end of the Arkansas Riot Case, was for law and order, peace, the efficient running of the machine. To whites in power the most valuable commodity was the retention of their power without successful opposition. Whatever the motives of the outsiders, and they were many, including compassion for the hell that Arkansas sharecroppers were living in economically, the fact remains that the Arkansas case was one where the outside world had more powerful and persuasive forces on its side than did the inside world of that castle-machine, Phillips County, Arkansas.

A great friend of cruelty is isolation, darkness, the mental and physical ignorance and impotence of the victim and of the rest of the world. The compact majority has a strong tendency to keep exerting its power for its own security. And when its actions are questioned, it can enlist language in their defense, words like "duty" and "Christian discipleship." These words may soften some of its own doubts, and the doubts of a few who are too weak to rise up; but to those who are in the stance of fighting back those words, in the language of that white moderate quoted above, get no response.

When a man is indulging in special pleading, pleading his own case in his own interest, it is astonishing how readily he comes up with defenses. His mind is suddenly fertile, bursting with reasons that favor his cause. Certainly his own felt necessity mothers his inventions. But when these words are pleading for the maiming of the lives of his audience, and when that audience is aroused, is feeling the painful joys of being active in its own interests and in its own ways, then those words fall still-born between the victimizer and his victims.

But in order for the victim to achieve this activity other than momentarily, in order for the victims to avoid indulging in the Sadean pleasures of perverse, episodic, orgasmic cruelties which are soon crushed by immense resistance, the victims, powerless individually in the castle-machine, must both organize themselves and get help from the outside. Without this organization and this help there are only episodic, futile reactions that can give the erstwhile victim momentary pleasure, and lingering death. With this organization forces arise that have their own momentum, their own continuity, their own history. And when the power of the victim and his allies, when the power of active human beings is great enough, the victim becomes visible and audible, a solid resistance. Without that active power, the many devices men use to disregard the lives of passive, powerless victims come into play.

The physiological fact is that our nerves are within our own respective skins; we feel most poignantly the crushing of our own lives, not the crushing of the lives of others. Or if we see what is happening to others, we are so ingenious, and so well-equipped by civilization or culture to "justify" what we are doing that we can live with that "terrible crushing and grinding," and go about our smoothly efficient everyday lives inside the machine of slavery or Jim Crow or peonage.

The issue is not only fear—that the victim must make the victimizer fearful if he is to pour water on the fire of his delirium or put sand in his machinery; the question is one of *perception*. The victimizer must see and feel his erstwhile victim as a resisting person.

There is an old American story that summarizes this. A man was trying to drive his mule across a bridge and was whipping him with a stick. Another man came up to him and said, "That's no way to get him to move. Let me try." And so the owner stepped back, and the newcomer seized a large block of wood and hit the mule over the head with it . . . .

"Why, you told me that the stick was no way of doing it," said the owner.

"Well," said the other, "you see I had to get his *attention* first." The question is one of attention, not sentimental, episodic, occasional attention, but sustained, effective attention. We have been noticing that we can maim and be maimed without important resistance, without being forced to see what is happening to the victim.

A castle-machine must be fought by a power that has some of the castle's characteristics: it must intensify and focus the mental and physical activities of the victim, and it must keep the victimizer from finding allies or from organizing and focusing his forces. It must even project stereotypes onto the faces of the victimizers.[73]

But the passivity of the victim helps the machine run smoothly, helps keep the lord of the castle at liberty to torture and crush that victim. In fact, there seems to be evidence for passivity being a stimulus to cruelty. Certainly passivity is essential to the successful operation of all kinds of cruelty. If slum dwellers are not active, if laborers are not active, if America's Indians are not active, or if the Negroes are not active, then not only will they fail to get allies from the outside, but they will in their passivity encourage their victimizers.

Still it has always taken a great deal of moral and even physical power to smash a machine built on sheer power. It is plain not only from the United States Civil War itself, but from the history of anti-slavery movements before that war that the victimizer will usually not initiate the smashing of the machine that gives him leisure, wealth, status. The initiative usually comes from an alliance between the victims and outsiders. The Quakers and many others combined to destroy slavery in America. The planters—except for very rare cases like that of James G. Birney—did nothing to destroy it. As long as their castle walls were intact and the machine was grinding profitably and smoothly, moral and religious laws could be bent to fit their interests. One of William Lloyd Garrison's telling phrases, "danger and guilt," summarizes this: it takes both, not simply guilt, which is slow and erratic in its rising, to remedy cruelty of any sort. And the guilt often *follows* the sense of danger, the feeling that the lord's dominion will be shattered by the erstwhile victim. Danger has produced some very moral thoughts and actions and has made men speak against their interests when those interests begin to involve the power of the erstwhile victim. James Farmer, one of the founders of CORE, tells the story of the Negro sharecropper who was plowing a field with his mule one day when a white motorist came up and rather rudely asked directions to a nearby town. When the black man failed to respond to the imperious "Boy, I'm askin' you a question!" the white man became abusive. Thereupon, the Negro whipped a competent-looking pistol out of his pocket and pointed it at his tormenter, suggesting that the white man might want to kiss his mule. "You know," said the white man, "I've always *wanted* to kiss a mule!"

As we have noticed, there is a curious kind of innocence in institutional and even in personal cruelty; great institutions do not often give as their rationale the desire to maim. Their rationale lies often in other things—like riches, purity of race, etc. And personally cruel persons can, for various reasons, say and mean "This hurts me more than it hurts you, but it has to be done," as those fathers in Hogarth's first plate of the *Marriage* might readily aver. Both of these kinds of cruelty can hide the face of the victim from the victimizer, can make the victim passive and the victimizer active, for the victim's "own sake." But when the face becomes a force, when it can be "seen" in all the ways people can "see" people, then the cruel relationship can be changed. But the point of this book is that it is not a purely theoretical or intellectualistic "seeing" that is involved: it is a total seeing of a human being or of a group of human beings that can bring about the changing of that relationship. Fully "seeing" the portrait of Frederick Douglass that is opposite this page involves, of course, reading his autobiography; and once this is done, it becomes very difficult indeed to think of him as a "victim" of the cruel relationship. He was hurt by it, but at an early age he stopped being passive within it, and in so doing he presented himself to his would-be victimizers and his own allies as a total human force, outside of the cruel relationship. The moral, intellectual, and physical power of a particular human being or of a group of particular human beings is more formidable and more dependable than the force of an abstract law or rationale.

Still, to say this is not yet to have rounded out our picture of cruelty and its resistance. The Arkansas riot and the contests that followed it are on too large a scale to exhibit this picture as far as the *personal experience* of the victim is concerned. Large numbers of people were involved in the Arkansas case, and besides, the experience of the victim himself as an individual resisting does not appear clearly in the records. Perhaps in the battles that followed the riot, outsiders (including attorney U.S. Bratton and so many other persons and organizations) did too much, and thereby obscured the ability of the victim himself to put his own "personal grain of sand into the smooth machinery." Anyway, to conclude this chapter, let us turn to a book we have already used to help illustrate the suffering of the victim and his resistance to the victimizer, *The Life and Times of Frederick Douglass*.

Frederick Douglass

Frederick Douglass (then named Frederick Augustus Washington Bailey) was born in February, 1817, in eastern Maryland, the son of a white man and a slave mother. Like all slaves Douglass was raised with two mutually related forces at work upon his mind: first, there was what he called "slaveholding priestcraft." He was

> Trained from the cradle up to think and feel that . . . masters were superiors, and invested with a sort of sacredness, there were few who could rise above the control which that sentiment exercized.[74]

According to this training, God was the author of slavery and the relationship between master and slave was a merciful, beneficial one—a paradise compared to the horrors they had been saved from by being removed from Africa. Their hard hands and dark color were a plain sign of God's displeasure with them, and slavery was the most beneficent way for them to live under that displeasure. The will of their God-given white masters was then comparatively benign punishment. The consequence of all this was that any attempt to escape from slavery or resist it was an offense "against God and man." The slaveholder participated in the sacredness of God, and so did the slave relationship; to try to break or hinder it was to break or hinder one's relationship to God in His infinite goodness.

The second "sentiment" which exercised control over the slaves was

> . . . a belief in the boundlessness of slave territory, and of their own [the slaveholders'] limitless power . . . [75]

A tremendous force, whose main purpose was to keep them in their sacred relationship with the slaveholder, surrounded them, a force that isolated them physically, as well as spiritually, from any possibility of escape or resistance. In one of the most penetrating and eloquent pages in his autobiography Douglass tells how slaves saw blood and misery around them "feeding upon our flesh," and in the very far distance

> . . . shadows under the flickering light of the North Star, behind some craggy hill or snow-capped mountain, stood a doubtful freedom, half-frozen, and beckoning us to her icy domain.[76]

And the freedom was "doubtful" because they did not know exactly what was beyond the apparently "boundless" slave territory surrounding them. At least they knew about their chances for survival *here*, in this misery and bloodshed. But as for what surrounded them

> The reader can have little idea of the phantoms which would flit . . . before the uneducated mind of the slave. Upon either side we saw grim death, assuming a variety of horrid shapes. Now it was starvation, causing us, in a strange and friendless land, to eat our own flesh. Now we were contending with the waves and were drowned. Now we were hunted by dogs and overtaken, and torn to pieces by their merciless fangs. We were stung by scorpions, chased by wild beasts, bitten by snakes, and, worst of all, after having succeeded in swimming rivers, encountering wild beasts, sleeping in the woods, and suffering hunger, cold, heat, and nakedness, were overtaken by hired kidnappers, who, in the name of the law and for the thrice-cursed reward, would . . . capture all.[77]

And Douglass says:

> . . . This dark picture, drawn by ignorance and fear, at times greatly shook our determination.[78]

Phantoms based on reality helped weaken their will to live as free men—and weakened that will by paralyzing the slave between *amor et timor*.

What was there that could brush these images from the brain and free the slave, at least from the images? The story of how Douglass finally escaped from slavery gives the answer for a particular man. Because he was a person with an irresistible desire to see facts fit together consistently, he started finding discrepancies between those images and the facts. For instance, he found it very difficult indeed to see Aunt Esther, a beautiful young slave, whipped mercilessly again and again simply for loving another slave. This, he said was in conflict with the idea

> . . . that God was good, and that He knew what was best for everybody. . . . It came point blank against all my notions of goodness.[79]

Uncertainties, the same thoughts that we have described as central to the cruelty of the black situation in America, the same thoughts that young people of all times have had in their struggle for consistency, these helped smash the images that bound the slave Frederick to his masters. Doubt, basically, is insistent conflict between beliefs; Douglass's doubts started the work of liberating him from the images.

But not only moral considerations raised these doubts. The idea that "God up in the sky" had made this whole system began to seem unfounded in fact. As he put it, "I could not tell how anybody could know that God made black people to be slaves."[80] He could find no evidence for this belief. Moreover, he could find evidence that not all black people were slaves, and that not all white people were masters. The omnipotence of the white man over the black was *as a fact* dubious when he witnessed a certain incident:

> My Aunt Jennie and one of the men slaves of Captain Anthony ran away. A great noise was made about it. Old master was furious. He said he would follow them and catch them and bring them back, but he never did, and somebody told me that Uncle Noah and Aunt Jennie had gone to the free states and were free.[81]

And not only did slaves escape through the ring of tremendous force that was supposed to surround them:

> ... several slaves on Mr. Lloyd's place ... remembered being brought from Africa. There were others who told me that their fathers and mothers were stolen from Africa.[82]

Man had made slavery! Man, with all his fallibility, had made it. From all the conflicts, there came toward the end of Douglass's mental pilgrimage out of slavery the following conviction:

> My faculties and powers of body and soul are not my own, but are the property of a fellow-mortal in no sense superior to me, except that he has the physical power to compel me to be owned and controlled by him. By the combined physical force of the community I am his slave—a slave for life.[83]

Of course this realization did not come from sheer intellectual doubts; it came from trying out in action the belief in his own "faculties and powers of body and soul." Learning how to read and write started the process, but Douglass tells us that it was a particular incident that culminated it.

Because he was a difficult slave to order around, he was sent to a certain Covey, known in the region as "The Negro Breaker." Covey was not a bold, big man like Simon Legree; he was a serpent-like creature, who would sneak up on his slaves by crawling in tall grass or behind obstacles, and he would leap on them with his lash when they were totally unaware. He was, in Douglass's words, "a wretch whose character for revolting cruelty beggars all opprobrious speech."[84] Covey so tortured the young man by his unpredictable (and thereby indefinitely threatening) behavior and by whippings and kicks in the body with his heavy boots that Douglass with the North Star glimmering faintly in his thoughts ran away.

He ran to his owner, Master Thomas,

> ... my professedly *Christian* master, humbly to invoke the interposition of his power and authority, to protect me from further abuse and violence. . . .[85]

And then occurred that sequence of feelings that every perceptive slave became accustomed to seeing in his master's eyes: first he was "somewhat affected by the story of my wrongs"; then he "repressed whatever feeling he may have had and became as cold and hard as iron . . . ."[86] What Douglass was witnessing was one man's Christianity and simple personal compassion crumbling "before the systematic tyranny of slavery." After walking the floor a bit before the bleeding young man,

> He began moderately by finding excuses for Covey, and ended with a full justification of him, and a passionate condemnation of me. He had no doubt I deserved the flogging. He did not believe I was sick—I was only endeavoring to get rid of work. My dizziness was laziness and Covey did right to flog me as he had done.[87]

The still energetic young man tried to answer these arguments with arguments—but the indefinite charge of "impudence" hung over his head, one verbal form that his weakness took in the slave-master relationship.

The fact was that if young Frederick permanently left Covey before his allotted full year was expired, his *"brother in the church,"* Frederick's master, would lose his slave's wages for the whole year. And so that other verbal form of his weakness, "laziness" was used on the young man. In a relationship wherein there were no permanent rewards or esteem for doing well, and no motive for laboring except the lash

> The charge of laziness against the slaves was ever on their lips and was the standing apology for every species of cruelty and brutality.[88]

Impudence and laziness were the images in the slaveholder's mind that helped justify anything—even the destruction of his own property, the slave. To argue against these massive images and the realities they rounded out for the slaveholder was for Douglass exactly like trying "to reason with bears and tigers."[89] The moral laws, the spiritual attitudes, the specific actions that Christianity praised, the very powers of reasoning themselves were nothing under the force of the system and the unlimited power—physical and mental—that the white slaveholder had over the slave. From Frederick's youthful point of view, that of scepticism, reason in these matters was what Montaigne in his *Apology for Raymond Sebond* called

> ... an instrument of lead and of wax, stretchable, pliable, and adaptable to all biases and all measures. ... [90]

The power of reasoning was twisted into a special shape by the powers of imagination, by self-interest, and by the ascendancy the slave system gave to the slaveholder. Frederick saw all this with his many-levelled mind, and the next day he returned to Covey. That "conversation" with Master Thomas was a mental hammer Frederick was using and was going to use to shatter the last vestiges of the imagery that bound him to his "sacred" master.

He went back to Covey on a Sunday, when he knew Covey would not harm him because Covey kept the Sabbath. But Monday came, and while Frederick, still recuperating from Covey's old blows (though having rested two days) was getting ready to feed and get ready the horses

> Covey sneaked into the stable, in his peculiar way, and seizing me suddenly by the leg, he brought me to the stable floor, giving my newly-mended body a terrible jar.[91]

At this moment came Douglass's real birth into freedom from those images and from the system: *he fought back.* A few days ago he would have trembled under Covey's slightest verbal threat "Like a leaf in a storm," like the victim of an indefinite power in a horror tale; but "I was resolved to fight, and what was better still, I actually was hard at it." He threw the snake-like Covey to the manure-covered floor, flat on his back, and in the midst of the struggle, when Covey, trembling, asked him "Are you going to resist, you scoundrel?" he answered with "a polite 'Yes, sir.' "[92] That reply expressed the core of Frederick's new found certainty, a certainty he was never to lose, a certainty that made him free.

While Covey was on his back in the manure, a slave named Bill came up and refused Covey's command to take hold of Frederick with the words "My master hired me here to work, and not to help you whip Frederick." And when Frederick said to Bill "don't put your hands on me," Bill replied "My God, Frederick, I ain't goin' to tech ye." Then comes an amazing statement in Douglass's account:

> During the whole six months that I lived with Covey after this transaction, he never again laid the weight of his finger on me in anger.[93]

Frederick had drawn blood from Covey, but Covey had not drawn blood from Frederick. The power relationship—amazingly enough, in that time and place—was changed in the minds and bodies of these two men. The boy had effectively removed himself—in what was to prove a permanent way—from the relationship of cruelty, at least with regard to this white man. In the minds of these two men facing each other as individuals, the machine was broken, Poe's pendulum had stopped moving down upon the victim, though the victim was still caught in the dungeon.

Douglass summarizes his reflections on that relationship as follows:

> This battle with Mr. Covey ... was the turning point in my "life as a slave." It rekindled in my breast the smouldering embers of liberty. It brought up my Baltimore dreams [when he had been learning how to read in a peaceful, affectionate household] and revived a sense of my own manhood. I was a changed being after that fight. I was nothing before—I was a man now. It recalled

to life my crushed self-respect and my self-confidence, and inspired me with a renewed determination to be a free man.[94]

Then he explains why Covey did not hurt him any more, and why Bill had not helped Covey:

A man without force is without the essential dignity of humanity. Human nature is so constituted that it cannot honor a helpless man, though it can pity him, and even this it cannot do long if signs of power do not arise.[95]

A purely passive, literally dead man is buried or cremated by the living. A figuratively or imaginatively dead man is ignored by his torturers and by his fellow victims. Covey and Bill could no longer ignore the "victim"—he was *real* to them, active, alive, and his reality took the form of resolved, certain, steady, effective resistance, a form perhaps dreamt of by Sade, but feared by him, and certainly a form feared by the slaveholders.

Douglass was free not only of the images, and in fact of the immediate effect of his action, because Covey became "as gentle as a lamb"; he was free from a deeper fear, the fear of death. And it was this freedom, so similar to the freedom expressed by Patrick Henry in his "Give me liberty or give me death" oration, that as Douglass puts it "made me a freeman in *fact.*"[96]

This brings us to an important point that Douglass's story and our general account in this chapter have not emphasized enough: the risks of running away, let alone of resisting a white man physically, were immense. *Father Henson's Story*, to which we have referred, was more explicit about those dangers than was Douglass's account.[97] Henson shows how the mere sentence "A nigger has struck a white man" was enough to inflame a whole county with rage and "no question is asked about the provocation." The slaveowner, or other whites, could kill the black man on the spot, with no fear of reprisals or prosecution. Another man than Covey might have killed Douglass instead of staying away from him; Covey did not own Douglass and so might have felt loathe to destroy another's property. The poor-white "patrols," the guns, the hounds, the swamps, and the vast legal powers the white man had over the black all made it extremely dangerous for a man to fight back or to try to escape. If he weren't hurt immediately, he could be sent down to a living hell in the land of King Cotton, the deep south, and could be separated from his loved ones in the process, hurting them as well as himself.

Positive courage as well as desperation ("What have I got to lose if I am *nothing?*") might cause a man to run these risks, but it is foolishly romantic to think that he could readily resist or escape enslavement. The fact that there were so many rebellions is—even given this desperation and raw courage—remarkable. It shows many things, but it also shows how horrible slavery must have been, that many should risk life to escape it.

Still, as some of the preceding remarks have implied, we must not over-emphasize the physical risks of resistance. As was hinted at in our study of the Gothic Tale, the decision to resist or escape is itself a kind of freedom from the victimizer. As Douglass put it:

> When a slave cannot be flogged, he is more than half free. He has a domain as broad as his own manly heart to defend, and he is really "a power on earth."[98]

He may knowingly risk death, but taking that risk cuts out for him, no matter what the external circumstances, an area in which he is free, because he is deciding something independently of his victimizer, or rather in spite of his victimizer; he is creating his own "domain," his own area wherein he can exert the power to decide. And he may be killed, but while he lives he lives not on his back or on his knees, but on his feet. A full understanding of the victim's resistance requires us to see both the external risks he runs and the internal joys he experiences; failing to see either element is failing to see the whole nature of resistance to an oppressor.

We need not here relate how Douglass left the dungeon by turning his "steps toward the North Star till we reached a free state." Nor need we study his personal and public relationships with Harriet Beecher Stowe and the two great Abolitionists, John

Brown and William Lloyd Garrison. And we need not consider the publication of his newspaper *The North Star*. We have already seen in general what the allies of the erstwhile victims can do to remove the remaining fragments of images that keep men in the cruel relationship.

And only a separate book could treat with any care the motivations of Douglass's allies. When one thinks of the Abolitionists on the one hand—William Lloyd Garrison and John Brown, for instance—and the American Colonization Society on the other—Daniel Webster and James Madison, for example—one is thinking of a variety of approaches and of men that is very great. Webster was a man who could defend the Fugitive Slave Law that Harriet Beecher Stowe, and certainly every slave, so despised; and the differences proliferate the more closely one studies these many powerful creatures. This is not even to dwell upon the deepest difference of all: the Abolitionist goal of immediate freedom for the slaves and the Colonization goal of sending them back to Africa. In the presence of all these differences, one can only say with Montaigne, on vast issues, "It is always man we are dealing with" not any single motivation that one can state abstractly and conclusively.

This complexity gets even greater when we try to answer the question: why do allies of the victim arise at all? In the first plate of Hogarth's *Cruelty* engravings, one boy, the one offering the tart to Nero, feels simple compassion, "feeling for those in bonds as bound with them," to use W.L. Garrison's phrase;[99] the other, drawing the gallows, believes in threats, like Hogarth himself. But whatever the motivations and justifications for such help, they are in all likelihood so various that here too we can only say, "It is always man we are dealing with."

But with all these complexities of personality and motivation, we must not lose sight of a force that the most effective allies of the victims displayed. Their force of *conviction* matched the force of the young Frederick in his battle with Covey, though it involved more factors than did this personal battle. In a crucial chapter of Douglass's autobiography, the one entitled "John Brown and Mrs. Stowe," he tells of a conversation with Brown in Springfield, Massachusetts, in 1847, while Douglass was trying to make up his mind about the methods most appropriate to the abolition of slavery. Somewhat taken aback by Brown's military plans for invading the system, Douglass demurred:

> "But you might be surrounded and cut off from your provisions or means of subsistence." He thought that this could not be done so they could not cut their way out, but even if the worst came he could but be killed, and he had no better use for his life than to lay it down in the cause of the slave. When I suggested we might convert the slaveholders, he became much excited, and said that could never be, he knew their proud hearts and that they would never be induced to give up their slaves, until they felt a big stick about their heads. He observed that I might have noticed the simple manner in which he lived, adding that he had adopted this method in order to save money to carry out his purposes. . . . Had some men made such display of rigid virtue, I would have rejected it, as affected, false, and hypocritical, but in John Brown, I felt it to be real as iron or granite.[100]

Certainly what some in those days called "fanaticism" was what many of the allies exhibited in their efforts to break the system of slavery. And it took various forms, including the form of journalism. Garrison's first issue of *The Liberator* had appalled many scholars and slaveholders with its words published on January 1, 1831,

> I *will* be as harsh as truth, and as uncompromising as justice. On this subject I do not wish to think, or speak, or write, with moderation. No! No! tell a man whose house is on fire, to give a moderate alarm; tell him to moderately rescue his wife from the hands of the ravisher; . . . but urge me not to use moderation in a cause like the present. I am in earnest—I will not equivocate—I will not excuse—I will not retreat a single inch—AND I WILL BE HEARD.[101]

At this time Garrison was an enemy of violence in the cause of abolishing slavery, and so his statement is one of absolute certainty and firmness of will, not a call to bloodshed, as were John Brown's remarks to Douglass. Earlier he had described his state of mind, and this description uses some of the language we have been using in this book:

> How do I bear up under my adversities? I answer—like the oak—like the Alps—unshaken, storm-proof. Opposition, and abuse, and

slander, and prejudice, and judicial tyranny, are like oil to the flame of my zeal. I am not dismayed; but bolder and more confident than ever. I say to my persecutors—I bid you defiance! Let the courts condemn me to fine and imprisonment for denouncing oppression: Am I to be frightened by dungeons and chains? Can they humble my spirit? . . . [102]

And the answer is No. Such certainty in the minds of erstwhile victims and allies was the main spiritual and personal source of **opposition to the victimizer and to his self-serving images. Scholars have contested the necessity for such severity** [103] **but our task** is not to solve this problem: our task is to describe the kind of personal force that some of the victims and some of their allies had in their resistance to victimization. That force was the force of certainty, the force of those not tortured with self-doubt. [104]

There remains, however, one important point, a point related to our notion of the *fascinosum* that the victim feels toward his victimizer. Because Douglass was so deeply an active man, physically and mentally, this *fascinosum*, this "smiling at the glittering death, as a child at some rare bauble," to use Poe's words in "The Pit and the Pendulum," was no great force in his life. Too early in that life he became too firmly resolved to be active—for him there was no bauble to admire with a child's smile.

Of course other slaves, less vigorous than himself, lay smiling under the bauble. And Douglass tells how slaveholders sometimes would deliberately give their slaves plenty of whiskey and plenty of time to enjoy momentary pleasures that resembled the pleasures of liberty. A slaveholder would run contests of various sorts, including drinking-contests, wherein the slave who could drink the most was rewarded—by a prize, and by his own bestial behavior. The purpose of these organized orgies was to disgust the slaves with their "temporary freedom," [105] so that they would be glad to return to work, as glad as they had been to leave it. And besides, they most salubriously became disgusted with *themselves* afterwards.

But none of this trapped Douglass. After the conversation with Master Thomas and the Covey fight he came to the conclusion that is one of the main contentions of this book. He put it this way:

> The kindness of the slave-master only gilded the chain. It detracted nothing from its weight or strength. The thought that men are for other and better uses than slavery throve best under the gentle treatment of a kind master.[106]

Then he uses the very word that translates *fascinosum;* with regard to kindness,

> Its grim visage could assume no smiles able to fascinate the partially enlightened slave into a forgetfulness of his bondage, or of the desirableness of liberty.[107]

One of the key contentions of this book is one of the key ideas of Douglass's autobiography: the opposite of cruelty is not kindness; nor is it Christian love (except if that word is subjected to what Montaigne would call "a long interpretation," an interpretation entirely in terms of the victim's point of view). *The opposite of cruelty is freedom.* The victim does not need the ultimately destructive gift of kindness when offered *within the cruel relationship.* He needs freedom from that relationship. He needs life, activity, a past upon which to build his confidence in the future, a present not stripped of power to move his body and his mind in his own way. He needs to find a way similar to the way other more fortunate men are moving their bodies, and their lives.

Once a man sees what is outside the castle and outside the machine, whether he sees it with Ellison's inner eye or with his own physical eyes, the images he may have been raised with start cracking and new completions of his experience start forming. Freedom, like slavery, is not "innate," not born with the mind of its possessor independently of all experience of the outer world. It is relative to that experience. It is quite likely that in certain societies slavery could be thought of as freedom—if the machine is smooth enough and the castle impregnable enough. Freedom from cruelty is freedom from the cruel person or society, but it is freedom that exists somewhere, if only in the mind or dreams of men.

Moreover, as much that has been said in this chapter implies, freedom *in general* is not guaranteed by a particular act of liberation. Poe's victim emerges from the machine, but he is still in the dungeon. Douglass emerged from the machine, and fled the dungeon; but the second half of his autobiography is darkened by the shadows of slavery in America. To remove oneself from one cruel relationship is not to remove oneself automatically from all. Douglass stayed free during the remainder of his life in the North by each day refusing to endure the condition of weakness under active strength. He could have summarized his whole life, not only his life in slavery, with Goethe's phrase: "Each man earns his freedom and existence by each day conquering them anew." Just as the agent of cruelty is a particular agent—though it may be vast and indefinite, or may be a particular person in a strong situation—so the absence of cruelty, freedom from the cruel agent, is a particular absence, a particular freedom. To remain free is a continuing battle against particular threatening agents.

All of this is to say in a somewhat extended form what Byron had said in the second book of *Childe Harold* (a saying beloved by Douglass):

Who would be free, themselves must strike the blow.

The agent of the cruel relationship, the victimizer, does not give freedom by being kind, as we have noticed. When Douglass's master did little kindnesses for him, like giving him a few cents of the many dollars Douglass had earned for him, Douglass thought that this

> . . . was proof that he suspected I had a right to the whole of them, and I always felt uncomfortable after having received anything in this way, lest his giving me a few cents might possibly ease his conscience, and make him feel himself to be a pretty honorable robber after all.[108]

What is well-intentioned kindness to the victimizer can be torture to the victim. A loving but dominating mother can torture her son with her kindness as destructively as a master can torture his slave with it. The gilding on the chain adds to its weight; it certainly does not lighten it—except, perhaps, when the slave is too tired, and too grateful for little favors to be a Douglass.

Of course manumission could be a kindness that was not in itself a torture to the victim. But not only was this legalistic "freedom" infrequently given and precariously maintained, especially in the South (as we have noticed); this kind of freedom was superficial compared to the freedom we have been discussing. For us freedom from slavery has meant liberation from the power-situation and from the images that have enslaved the Negro in America. But a negative statement does not describe fully this deeper freedom. A man requires that the situation and the images that once made him a thing be replaced by a new situation and by new images; he needs definite ideals that *he* desires to pursue, and he needs a situation that permits him to pursue them as successfully as his abilities permit.

These are clichés, hackneyed phrases in the American creed. It is for the black man and for his allies to make them descriptions of fact.

And so, unlike the Gothic Tale, these three hundred years of cruelty may not be consummated in a way that will give us Kermode's "sense of an ending." Aside from the subtle and complex nature of the struggle that has been going on in America all these years, there are specific dangers that may keep us from having this consummatory peace. Many of the black people may become daunted or wearied by the immense power of the economic, political, and military establishment; then the old cruelties would continue. Or many white people may become passive or desperately fearful; then new cruelties would appear, sometimes perpetrated by the desperate white majority, sometimes perpetrated by the powerful black minority. Or many black people may become so revengeful about the past and its shadows in the present that they will strike out desperately and futilely against all whites and do nothing to change the economic and political power situation in this country.

But since the struggle of the black people for this deeper freedom is being waged in all the dimensions of their spirit, there is hope that the shadows of slavery will be dispelled in America. And for the individual black person in America, the life of such a man as Frederick Douglass can be itself a significant season that can help him to find his own freedom from all those cruelties.

CONCLUSION

HERE is George Bernard Shaw's judgment on a familiar French maxim—it occurs in the Preface to *Saint Joan:*

> ... there was a great wrong done to Joan and to the conscience of the world by her burning. *Tout comprendre, c'est tout pardonner*, which is the Devil's sentimentality, cannot excuse it. When we have admitted that the tribunal was not only honest and legal, but exceptionally merciful in respect of sparing Joan the torture which was customary ... and that Cauchon was far more self-disciplined and conscientious both as a priest and lawyer than any English judge ever dreams of being in a political case in which his party and class prejudices are involved, the human fact remains that the burning of Joan of Arc was a horror, and that a historian who would defend it would defend anything.

Shaw was quite right in applying the maxim "To understand all is to pardon all" to a court case: pardon is, technically speaking, a matter for judges, juries, and other legal agents to decide, and the maxim assumes that the one who is doing the pardoning has an impartial, objective relationship to the harm-doing he is pardoning, the relationship, for example, of the ideal judge or jury. Of course it also assumes, as Shaw clearly sees, that it is the *victimizer* we are "comprehending," not the victim's destruction.

But when one is a participant in substantial cruelty, in agony unto death, this assumption of impartiality becomes questionable—an ideal, not something to be assumed. The dizzying implications of such questioning are nowhere more strikingly put than in Herman Melville's *Moby Dick* when Captain Ahab says to Mr. Starbuck: "Who's to doom when the judge himself is dragged to the bar?" It is very difficult to find an impartial judge on all-important matters, like matters of life and death. And *until we find that judge* we must try to comprehend the participants' points of view, both the one whose pardon is being discussed and the one who has suffered.

Like Shaw's play, this book has dealt with both the victimizer's and the victim's point of view. And even this broadly-stroked sketch shows that the victim and the victim's allies have nothing to do with exoneration—their task is to suffer or fight back. With regard to them pardon is an inapplicable metaphor the Devil might use to tempt his victims to succumb. In fact, the more one sees the destruction that men can perpetrate on each other, the less one thinks of such an ideal as pardon. One thinks of vengeance; one thinks of reparation; one thinks of reform; one thinks of many things, but not pardon: even Sade's powerless victims cannot pardon their victimizers.

The image of destructive power, the Devil, the vastly daemonic opposite of God's creativity, has much glamor, much enchantment for us weak creatures. The infernal version of the *mysterium tremendum et fascinosum* draws our interest—in fact, he can be so interesting that his victims can be forgotten. We can fear and admire him and his power while we ignore what that power does to the victim, and what the victim can do against that power. And the same applies to small tempters and destroyers; it is very easy to forget the sufferer, perhaps because there is less glamor or enchantment in suffering than there is in action.

But whatever the reasons, moral laws tend to focus on the powerful active ones more than they do on the re-active or passive ones. And the same applies to much of our ordinary language. For instance, in March's massive *Thesaurus Dictionary* the antonym of cruelty is charitableness or charity, and kindliness. And "charity" is defined as "generosity to the poor." But as we have seen in our study of Frederick Douglass's flight from slavery, these condescending words do not describe its opposite from the victim's point of view. Episodes of kindliness can exacerbate the tortures of the cruel relationship. When the victim sees that smug face lighting up with self-satisfaction after the sop has been thro wn, he undergoes a torture more exquisite than the straightforward tortures of that relationship. Institutional cruelty is not relieved by episodes of kindness—it is a continuing relationship, a continuing torture, at least from the sufferer's point of view. The only relief from it is freedom from that relationship. The victim's freedom to act—to fight back or escape—is *his* heart's desire. He needs no gilding on the chain. He needs to break the chain.

The reason why the Golden Rule is useful is that it hints (though from the would-be victimizer's point of view) at this freedom. "Do unto others as you would have others do unto you" hints at the victim's mode of awareness, at his freedom to act as he wishes; and it also hints at the *danger* the victimizer incurs when he forgets that the victim can be a force. Freedom for the victim is danger for the victimizer—the victim's freedom involves the overthrow of the dominion of the lord. And one of the reasons moral laws and rules are often things of wax, again to use Montaigne's metaphor, is that the danger of destroying, the total personal danger involved in maiming another human being, is simplified into the legalistic metaphor of "guilt." Danger and guilt must exist together in the victimizer's mind or he may not see what he is doing, just as Sade did not see his victims as real forces. Moral laws, until The Judge comes, if he ever could come, are simplifications "subject to a long interpretation," as Montaigne would put it. And that interpretation must always include the victim's need for autonomy.

It is appropriate, therefore, to look at history and the arts for a rounding-out of our understanding of the cruel relationship; legalistic and moralistic formulas assume an impartiality that is difficult to find, and they readily become wax in the hands of those powerful enough to put them into effect. In the resistance men make to their own destruction we see the beginning of an answer to Ahab's question, "Who's to doom when the judge himself is dragged to the bar?" The victim dooms—or at least he stands up and is seen and heard.

On such matters as we have been discussing, we should seek impartiality; we should seek the kind of moral guidance that gives us a fuller understanding of both the agent and the sufferer, lest we escalate cruelty by creating new victims. But we must not assume impartiality at the beginning. If we face the victim's face and force we make a step in the direction of an ideal understanding that does not blandly pardon but sees destruction for what it is.

If we can replace the "I-it" relationship between the victimizer and his victim with the intimate but threatening "I-you" relationship to a personal force, then we can hope to avoid the Devil's sentimentality. Seeing more facts is the best cure for any sentimentality.

The fact is that men are very dangerous to each other. They can at once want and not want to harm each other mortally. The heightened awareness of all the forms of this the paradox of cruelty can help us to understand and diminish the terrible waste of human life, and can bring us to moral wisdom, which is a sad wisdom, but not empty of hope.

POSTSCRIPT TO CRUELTY

A decade after writing *Cruelty* I found it incomplete—true, but not true enough. It had ignored, or at least slighted, certain important facts in history. I had written it as a skeptic, in the tradition of the Greek *skeptikoi* or "inquirers into facts." As a skeptic I had tried to avoid highfalutin abstractions that were too far above the ground-level particulars of human history. Many of the ancient skeptics were doctors trying to find ways of curing people of particular diseases, and they turned their backs upon the philosophers who studied their own abstract words instead of the facts of anatomy and medication. What their famous "doubt" was directed at was the philosophers' stratospheric book-battles about such very uncommon common nouns as "goodness" and "reality." They and their modern descendants Montaigne and Wittgenstein wanted to look into the patterns among facts not in order to find "The Truth" but in order to cope, in order to survive in a world of facts.

In this spirit I wrote *Cruelty*. Being a student of ethics I was concerned with evil, but being a skeptic I was more concerned with more ordinary words than "evil", words that turn up often in history and literature. "Cruelty" is such a word, and in studying patterns among the facts that illustrated cruelty I found certain patterns, the most basic being an imbalance of power between the victimizer and the victim. Like the old medical skeptics, I felt that by understanding these lower level abstractions I could help myself (at least) to cope with certain important facts.

But if cruelty is one of the main evils of human history, why is the opposite of cruelty not one of the main goods of human history? Such terms as "good" and "evil" are polar terms—they help define each other, the way "light" helps us to understand what we mean by "dark". In the years after writing *Cruelty* I grew to believe that the opposite of the evil that I had discussed in the book was not necessarily good. Though cruelty is important to what philosophers and theologians have called "evil," the mere cessation of cruelty, freedom from it, is not important to what they have called "good". Escape is a negative affair; goodness has something positive about it, sometimes even something triumphantly affirmative about it. I had failed to deal with the opposite of cruelty, and so my whole explanation of it lacked something important, important at least for a student of good *and* evil. In fact I had left out goodness.

By emphasizing the power of the victim I was making freedom from cruelty something that could be achieved by cruelty—freedom was not necessarily "good". I came to see that I had analyzed cruelty too exclusively in terms of sheer power, and power can be an instrument for good or evil, for the preservation or destruction of life. My discussion did not yet fit into ethics.

These misgivings prompted me to explore a level of ethics that skeptics usually avoid, the understanding of good and evil in terms of ethical laws or rules. I found that when you look at the ethical magnates of history you see in their words and deeds two kinds of ethical injunctions: negative and positive. The negative rules are scattered throughout the Bible but Moses brought down from Mount Sinai the main negative laws of the West: Thou shalt not murder; thou shalt not bear false witness. ... The positive injunctions are similarly spread across the pages of the Bible. In the first chapter of the book of Isaiah, for instance, we are told to ". . . defend the fatherless, plead for the widow. . . ." The negative ethic forbids certain types of actions; the positive demands certain types of actions.

To follow the negative ethic you need only clean hands, not active ones. The negative laws make up the ethic of decency: even an incompetent or a corpse can abide by them by doing nothing! But to follow the positive ethic, to be one's brother's keeper, is to be more than decent; it is to be active, even agressive. It involves going out of one's way for another. If the negative ethic is one of decency, the positive one is one of riskful, strenuous nobility. If the negative ethic is minimal, the positive ethic is maximal.

When I looked back at what I had written in *Cruelty* I saw that I had been thinking more about the ethics of decency than about the ethics of nobility. The prohibitions against murder, betrayal, and adultery are mainly prohibitions against cruelty. One could live a life without violating any of them, but so what? A minimal decent life is what John Milton was writing about in his *Areopagitica* when he deprecated ". . . a fugitive and cloister'd vertue, unexercis'd and unbreath'd, that never sallies out and sees her adversary, but slinks out of the race, where that immortall garland is to be run for, not without dust and heat. . . ." The decent ones who by incapacity are merely not cruel, or not evil, have, according to Milton ". . . but a blank vertue, not a pure; her whitenesse is but an excrementall whitenesse. . . ." If my work on cruelty had anything to do with goodness, it had to do only with the "excrementall whitenesse" of clean but useless hands.

And then one gray April afternoon while studying the French resistance to the Nazi occupants of France, a cruel way of fighting cruelty, I found a short factual account of the resistance activities of a French mountain village named Le Chambon-sur-Lignon. I shall not try to analyze here the tears of amazement and gladness and gratitude that I shed when I first read about these few incidents. Tears usually come from being overmastered, sometimes by sadness, sometimes by joy. The tears I felt on my cheeks by the time I had finished reading those few pages for the first time were tears of an almost wild joy. They were tears of awe that expressed my sudden knowledge that here in Le Chambon the best had happened. Goodness had happened. During the first four years of the 1940s, the time of the German occupation of France, this village of about three thousand people saved almost twice their number of refugees' lives without violence or the desire to be violent toward anyone.

They lived in accordance with both the positive and the negative ethical injunctions by not killing and by defending the fatherless. At first they saved mostly the children of parents who had been sent to the killing camps of Central Europe, but later in the occupation they began to rescue whole families.

There in Hitler's Fortress Europe most people—including myself as a combat artilleryman—found it easy, even inspiring to violate the negative laws of decency in the name of being our brothers' keepers. We killed in order to save, and so did most of the resisters who supported the Allies in Europe. And so did the Axis powers. But they chose not to sacrifice decency for a noble cause. In a maculate world they were immaculate—but theirs was no blank virtue. In his *Areopagitica* Milton makes a sharp distinction between a blank virtue and a pure one—theirs was pure because it was purified by trial, by action, by suffering, and by an unshakeable commitment to the weak.

The French Protestant village of Le Chambon is on the Lignon River in southeastern France. It is perched on a high plateau in the Cévennes Mountains. Under the puppet French government of Vichy, which was not only collaborating with the Nazi conquerors but was frequently trying to outdo the Germans in anti-semitism in order to please them, and later under the day-to-day threat of destruction by the Armed SS, they started to save children in the terrible winter of 1940, the winter after the fall of France. They continued to do so until the war in France was over in August of 1944. They sheltered the refugees and they took many of them across the dangerous mountains to neutral Switzerland (mainly to Geneva, whose Protestants cooperated with them). The people of Le Chambon are poor, and the Huguenot faith to which they belong is a diminishing faith in Catholic and atheist France; but their capacity to act in unison against the victimizers who surrounded them was immense. They were more than a match for their own government and for the conquerors of France.

For me they were the embodiment of the true opposite of cruelty. What they did for those refugees at such risk and for so long a period of time revealed to me not only a moment in history that was an instance of what John Milton had called the goodness of the "true wayfaring Christian," who is not satisfied with blank virtue; they also revealed to me that the polar opposite of cruelty is not simply release from that cruelty: it is hospitality.

The opposite of the cruelties of the killing camps of the Nazis was not the liberation of the camps, the cleaning out of the barracks and the cessation of the horrors. All of this was the end of the cruelty relationship, not necessarily its opposite. And that liberation was not even the end of it, because the victims would never forget and would remain in agony as long as they remembered their humiliation, their sufferings, and their loss. No, the opposite of cruelty was the kind of goodness that happened in the mountain village. And in learning this I learned to fit cruelty into ethics.

A letter I received from a woman who was saved by the village of Le Chambon makes the distinction between liberation and goodness clear. She wrote: ". . . Never was there a question that the Chambonnais would not share all they had with us, meager as it was. One Chambonnais once told me that even if there was less, they still would want more for us." And she went on to make the distinction clearer:

It was indeed a very different attitude from the one in Switzerland, which while saving us also resented us so much.

If today we are not bitter people like most survivors it can only be due to the fact that we met people like the people of Le Chambon, who showed to us simply that life can be different, that there are people who care, that people can live together, and even risk their own lives for their fellow man.

The Swiss helped liberate refugees; the people of Le Chambon did more. They taught them that goodness existed. The Chambon refugees have now taught their children this lesson, and in doing so they have helped them to have realistic hope in the possibility of goodness.

What was the nature of this hospitality that saved and deeply changed so many lives? The answer is hard to express briefly. The morning after a new refugee family came to town they would find on their front door a wreath with *"Bienvenue!"*

"Welcome!" painted on a piece of cardboard attached to the wreath. Nobody knew who had brought the wreath; in effect, the whole town had brought it.

One of the reasons the people of Le Chambon were successful in helping the refugees was that the Huguenots had been victims themselves. They had been persecuted for hundreds of years by the kings of France, and they knew how to cope with persecution. In fact, when the people of Le Chambon took Jewish children and later whole families across the mountains of southeastern France into Switzerland, they followed pathways that had been taken by Huguenots in their flight from the Dragoons of the French kings.

This much can be said about the hospitality of the Chambonnais: it was not self-conscious. When I asked them why they helped these, the most dangerous guests they could have had in Hitler's Fortress Europe, they invariably answered, "What do you mean, 'Why?' Where else could they go? How could we turn them away? Anyway, what is so special about being ready to help (*prêt à servir*)?" They would laugh in disbelief when I told them that I thought that they were good people. Helping these guests was *for them* as natural as breathing or eating. They did not think of alternatives to sheltering people who were endangering not only the lives of their hosts but also the lives of all the people of the village. The vast majority in France thought of alternatives: many Frenchmen ignored or betrayed or rejected refugees in those hard, humiliating years of the occupation. But for these people, for the Chambonnais, there was no interesting alternative to being "*prêt à servir*," ready to help.

What all of this means to me is that my attacks upon the idea that kindness is the opposite of cruelty have to be reconsidered and refined. I still believe what Douglass wrote about kindness: "The kindness of the slave-master only gilded the chain. It detracted nothing from its weight or strength. . . ."[1] The baubles victimizers sometimes give their victims in order to relieve their sense of guilt at small cost and in order to enslave their victims more deeply by passive gratitude or by self-hatred are not the opposite of cruelty. On the contrary, they are the perfection of cruelty. They finish the job, or rather keep the cruelty happening long after the violence has stopped. But what happened in Le Chambon was not this. What happened there was what I have rather hastily deprecated in the chapter, "The Black People and Groceries." What happened there was "Christian love." It was not the Christian love of Master Thomas, Douglass's master, whose compassion and religious convictions slowly and surely crumbled under the various pressures of slavery and under the subtler pressures of self-serving self-deception. What happened in Le Chambon was the kind of kindness that transforms the cruel relationship into a new relationship—that of unsentimental, riskful, costly help.

Le Chambon taught me that the defiance of a John Brown or of a William Lloyd Garrison has its place in history, but so does the help the Quakers gave the slaves by their hospitality on the path to the North Star. Like the Chambonnais they saw that of God in every man. They felt each person was as valuable as God, and they acted accordingly.

The goodness of such people is conciliatory, not adversarial, celebrative of life, not primarily defiant of the enemies of the weak. This goodness does not win wars, does not abolish slavery, does not change the history of nations and peoples—the adversaries are necessary to do this. In fact, without the Allies Le Chambon and its refugees would have been crushed eventually. The immaculate goodness of the Chambonnais has a limited effect in this nightmare we call history, but it has power, has its effects on the lives of those it touches. Cruelty truly ends only where conciliation, not defeat, truly begins.

Late in his *Life and Times* Frederick Douglass tells about his visits with the children of his former masters. He writes of his openhearted friendship with them after all those years of torture and struggle under slavery. And he writes:

If any reader of this part of my life shall see in it the evidence of a want of manly resentment for wrongs inflicted by slavery upon myself and race . . . so it must be. No man can be stronger than nature, one touch of which, we are told, makes all the world akin. I esteem myself a good, persistent hater of injustice and oppression, but my resentment ceases when they cease, and I have no heart to visit upon children the sins of their fathers.[2]

By taking this stand, Douglass not only stepped outside of the cruel relationship; he stood upon the grounds he cherished— the affirmation that when cruelty ceases it must cease in the minds of its former victims too. There must be a way of life that is not only retributively and equitably just, but cordial, hearty, like the hospitality of the Quakers and the Chambonnais, and like the affection Frederick Douglass felt for the children of his torturers. There must be an awareness of what he describes as "... nature, one touch of which, we are told, makes all the world akin. ...." Without that sense of communion we are not only in danger of perpetuating cruelty, but are in the even graver danger of failing to see why cruelty is an evil. It is an evil because it separates us into victims, victimizers, and spectators. It isolates us from each other. The alternative to that evil cannot be adversarial. The word "good" derives from certain early Teutonic and English words meaning "to gather" or "to unite," and the ideals of ethics have this meaning too. If ethics becomes only another excuse for combat, then the salt of life has lost its savor, and how shall its saltness be restored?

—January 1982

NOTES

INTRODUCTION TO THE PAPER EDITION

1. Frederick Douglass, *Life and Times* (Englewood Cliffs, N.J.: 1962), p. 155.
2. *Ibid.*, p. 395.

HOGARTH ON THE POWER OF THE WEAK

1. Georg Christoph Lichtenberg, *Lichtenberg's Commentaries on Hogarth's Engravings* (London, 1966), pp. 92–93.
2. Henry Fielding, *Joseph Andrews* (Middletown, Conn., 1967), p. 17.
3. William Hogarth, *The Analysis of Beauty* (Oxford, 1955), quotation from "Notes toward an autobiography" as found in the Appendix.
4. M. Dorothy George, *London Life in the Eighteenth Century* (Middlesex, 1965), p. 15.
5. William Hogarth, quoted from MS 49, British Museum.
6. *Op. cit.*, *The Analysis of Beauty*, p. 266.
7. *Op. cit.*, MS 49.
8. Max Weber as quoted in Arthur I. Waskow, *From Race Riot to Sit-In, 1919 and the 1960s* (Garden City, 1967), p. 2.

SADE AND THE MUSIC OF PAIN

1. D.A.F. de Sade, *Philosophy in the Bedroom*, in *The Marquis de Sade* (New York, 1966), p. 332.
2. *Ibid.*, p. 333.
3. *Ibid.*, p. 288.
4. *Ibid.*, p. 310.

5. See Sade's preface "To Libertines" at the head of *Philosophy in the Bedroom*, *Ibid.*, p. 185; see also his introduction to *The 120 Days of Sodom* (North Hollywood, 1967).
6. D.A.F. de Sade, *Juliette* (London, 1966), p. 299.
7. Sade, *Philosophy*, *op. cit.*, p. 185.
8. D.A.F. de Sade, "La Vérité," *Dialogue, Oxtiern, Ecrits politiques*, p. 120, in Vol. VIII *D.A.F. de Sade: Oeuvres complètes* (Paris, 1966). Translated by P.P. Hallie.
9. Sade, *Juliette*, *op. cit.*, p. 102.
10. *Ibid.*, p. 64.
11. *Ibid.*, p. 275.
12. *Ibid.*, p. 275.
13. D.A.F. de Sade, *Selected Letters* (London, 1965), p. 168.
14. D.A.F. de Sade, *The 120 Days of Sodom*, pp. 90–91.
15. Sade, *Juliette*, *op. cit.*, p. 108.
16. *Ibid.*, p. 35.
17. *Ibid.*, p. 38.
18. *Ibid.*, p. 128.
19. *Ibid.*, p. 53.
20. *Ibid.*, p. 101.
21. *Ibid.*, p. 31.
22. *Ibid.*, pp. 254–255.
23. Sade, *Philosophy*, *op. cit.*, p. 232.
24. See S. Kierkegaard, *Fear and Trembling*.
25. S. Kierkegaard, "Training in Christianity", *A Kierkegaard Anthology*, ed. Robert Bretall (New York, 1946), p. 409.
26. *Ibid.*, p. 287.
27. Louis-Ferdinand Céline, *Journey to the End of the Night* (London, 1966), p. 233.
28. *Ibid.*, p. 22.
29. *Ibid.*, p. 22.
30. D.A.F. de Sade, "Idée sur les romans," *Les Crimes de l'amour* p. 28, in Vol. III *D.A.F. de Sade: Oeuvres complètes* (Paris, 1961). Translated by P.P. Hallie.
31. *Ibid.*, p. 27.
32. *Ibid.*, p. 38.

HORROR AND THE PARADOX OF CRUELTY

1. Edith Birkhead, *The Tale of Terror* (New York, 1920).
2. Rudolph Otto, *The Idea of the Holy* (London, 1952), pp. 12–45.
3. Ann Radcliffe, *The Mysteries of Udolpho*, abridged in the collection *The Castle of Otranto; The Mysteries of Udolpho; Northanger Abbey*, ed. Andrew Wright (New York, 1963), p. 250.
4. Charles Robert Maturin, *Melmoth the Wanderer* (Lincoln, 1966), p. 22.

5. *Loc. cit.*
6. *Ibid.*, p. 247.
7. *Ibid.*, pp. 48–50.
8. Matthew G. Lewis, *The Monk* (New York, 1959), p. 45.
9. Maturin, *op. cit.*, p. 33.
10. *Ibid.*, p. 125.
11. Sheridan Le Fanu, *Carmilla*, in *The Vampire, and Anthology*, eds. Ornella Volta and Valeria Riva (London, 1965), p. 48.
12. Bram Stoker, *Dracula* (New York, 0000), p. 42.
13. Maturin, *op. cit.*, p. 160.
14. Mario Praz, "Introduction," *The Romantic Agony* (Cleveland, 1967), p. xiv.
15. Percy Bysshe Shelley, "Medusa," as quoted by Praz, *Ibid.*, p. 25.
16. Joseph Conrad, *Heart of Darkness*, in *A Conrad Argosy*, ed. William McFee (Garden City, 1942), p. 73.
17. Gustave Flaubert, cited by Praz, *op. cit.*, p. 159.
18. Friedrich Nietzsche, *The Genealogy of Morals*, in the collection *The Birth of Tragedy and The Genealogy of Morals* (Garden City, 1956), p. 184.
19. *Ibid.*, pp. 184–185.
20. Johann Peter Eckermann, *Conversations with Goethe* (London, 1946), p. 406.
21. Johann Wolfgang von Goethe, cited by Otto, *op. cit.*, p. 152.
22. Eckermann, *op. cit.*, p. 392.
23. Henry James, *The Turn of the Screw*, in *Ghostly Tales of Henry James*, ed. Leon Edel (New York, 1963), p. 337.
24. Stoker, *op. cit.*, p. 43.
25. Maturin, *op. cit.*, p. 358.
26. Lewis, *op. cit.*, p. 371.
27. Maturin, *op. cit.*, p. 231.
28. Lewis, *op. cit.*, pp. 419–420.
29. Frank Kermode, *The Sense of an Ending* (New York, 1967), p. 46.
30. Maturin, *op. cit.*, p. 197.
31. Lucretius, *On the Nature of Things*, in the anthology *The Stoic and Epicurean Philosophers*, ed. Whitney J. Oates (New York, 1940), p. 91.
32. *Cassell's New Latin Dictionary*, ed. D.P. Simpson (New York, 1959), p. 278.

FROM THE NOVEL TO HISTORY

1. Harriet Beecher Stowe, *Uncle Tom's Cabin, or, Life Among the Lowly* (New York, 1965), p. xxvii.
2. *Ibid.*, p. 371.
3. *Ibid.*, p. 374.
4. *Ibid.*, p. 403.

5. *Ibid.*, p. 404.
6. *Ibid.*, p. 444.

THE BLACK PEOPLE AND GROCERIES

1. Rudolf Vrba and Alan Bestic, *I Cannot Forgive* (England, 1964), p. 12.
2. *Ibid.*, p. 16.
3. D.A.F. de Sade, "La Vérité," *Dialogue, Oxtiern, Ecrits politiques*, p. 120, in Vol. VIII *D.A.F. de Sade; Oeuvres complètes* (Paris, 1966). Translated by P.P. Hallie.
4. Edgar Allan Poe, "The Black Cat," *Tales—Marvelous Adventure*, pp. 72–73, in Vol. VI of the commemorative edition of *The Works of Edgar Allan Poe* (New York, 1904).
5. Frantz Fanon, *The Wretched of the Earth*, trans. Constance Farrington (New York, 1968), p. 61.
6. *Ibid.*, p. 247.
7. Nancy Roelker, ed., *The Paris of Henry of Navarre* (Cambridge, 1968), p. 193.
8. Hannah Arendt, *Eichmann in Jerusalem* (New York, 1963), p. 79.
9. Frank Tannenbaum, *Slave and Citizen: The Negro in America* (New York, 1947), pp. 66–67. Tannenbaum is in turn quoting one George M. Stroud's *A Sketch of the Laws Relating to Slavery in America.*
10. See Tannenbaum's analysis, *Ibid.*, pp. 48–56.
11. *Ibid.*, p. 69.
12. *Ibid.*, pp. 68–71, *passim.*
13. Josiah Henson, *Father Henson's Story of His Own Life* (New York, 1962), p. 5.
14. Wilbur J. Cash, *The Mind of the South* (New York, 1941), pp. 82–83.
15. *Ibid.*, p. 84.
16. Harriet Beecher Stowe, *Uncle Tom's Cabin, or, Life Among the Lowly* (New York, 1965), p. 444.
17. Tannenbaum, *op. cit.*, p. 77.
18. Frederick Douglass, *Life and Times of Frederick Douglass; Written by Himself* (New York, 1962), pp. 37–38.
19. *Ibid.*, p. 38.
20. *Ibid.*, p. 39.
21. See W.E.B. Du Bois's essay, "Of the Dawn of Freedom," in his *The Souls of Black Folk* (Greenwich, Conn., 1967), pp. 23–41.
22. Gunner Myrdal, *An American Dilemma: The Negro Problem and Modern Democracy* (New York, 1944), p. 533 and *passim.*
23. *Ibid.*, p. 74.
24. *Ibid.*, p. 77.

25. See C. Vann Woodward, *The Strange Career of Jim Crow* (New York, 1957), pp. 51–52 and *passim.*
26. Douglass, *op. cit.,* pp. 224–225.
27. Rayford W. Logan, *The Negro in the United States: A Brief History* (Princeton, 1957), pp. 134–135.
28. Louis R. Harlan, *Separate and Unequal: Public School Campaigns and Racism in the Southern Seaboard States 1901–1915* (New York, 1968), pp. 12–15.
29. Woodward, *op. cit.,* p. 93.
30. Harlan, *op. cit.,* p. 222.
31. Solomon Northup, "Picking Cotton, . . ." in *In Their Own Words: A History of the American Negro, 1619–1865,* ed., Milton Meltzer (New York, 1967), pp. 39–40.
32. *Ibid.,* p. 40.
33. Douglass, *op. cit.,* p. 51.
34. *Ibid.,* p. 77.
35. *Ibid.,* p. 186.
36. *Ibid.,* p. 186.
37. *Ibid.,* p. 87.
38. Ralph Ellison, "Prologue," *The Invisible Man* (New York, 1965), p. 7.
39. *Ibid.,* p. 7.
40. W.E.B. Du Bois, *The Souls of Black Folk* (Greenwich, 1967), p. 16.
41. Douglass, *op. cit.,* p. 199.
42. Arendt, *op. cit.,* pp. 80–81.
43. Douglass, *op. cit.,* p. 244.
44. William H. Ferris, *The African Abroad* (New Haven, 1913), Vol. I, pp. 296–311.
45. Douglass, *op. cit.,* p. 145.
46. Tannenbaum, *op. cit.,* p. 4.
47. Douglass, *op. cit.,* p. 161.
48. For an extensive discussion of this aspect of *fascinosum,* see: Anna Freud, *The Ego and the Mechanisms of Defense* (London, 1948), p. 121 and *passim;* and Stanley M. Elkins, *Slavery: A Problem in American Institutional and Intellectual Life* (New York, 1963), pp. 115–133.
49. Harry Stack Sullivan, as quoted by Stanley M. Elkins, *Ibid.,* p. 122.
50. Theodore R. Sarbin, see Bibliography under Sarbin, T.R.
51. Du Bois, *op. cit.,* p. 16.
52. *Ibid.,* p. 17.
53. Myrdal, *op. cit.,* pp. 58, 69–70, 222, 431, 450, 452, 458, 540, 553, 560, 577–578, 602, 1338, *passim.*
54. *Supra,* Chapter Four: "Horror and the Paradox of Cruelty."

55. Charles Silberman, as quoted by Stokely Carmichael and Charles V. Hamilton in their *Black Power: The Politics of Liberation in America* (New York, 1967), p. 5.

56. Ernest Thompson Seton, "Pacing Mustang," in *Wild Animals I Have Known* (New York, 1946), p. 132.

57. Du Bois, *op. cit.*, p. 48.

58. *Ibid.*, p. 49.

59. *Ibid.*, p. 54.

60. Edgar Allan Poe, "The Pit and the Pendulum," *Tales—Marvelous Adventure*, p. 19, in Vol. VI of the commemorative edition of *The Works of Edgar Allan Poe.*

61. *Ibid.*, p. 24.

62. *Ibid.*, p. 27.

63. Arthur I. Waskow, *From Race Riot to Sit-In, 1919 and the 1960s* (Garden City, N.Y., 1967), pp. 121–174.

64. *Ibid.*, pp. 124–126.

65. *Ibid.*, p. 121.

66. *Ibid.*, p. 128.

67. *Ibid.*, p. 133.

68. *Ibid.*, p. 139.

69. *Ibid.*, p. 139.

70. *Ibid.*, p. 154.

71. *Ibid.*, p. 167.

72. *Ibid.*, p. 174.

73. See: Bruno Bettelheim, *The Informed Heart: Autonomy in a Mass Age* (New York, 1961), pp. 220–232.

74. Douglass, *op. cit.*, p. 145.

75. *Ibid.*, p. 161.

76. *Ibid.*, p. 162.

77. *Ibid.*

78. *Ibid.*

79. *Ibid.*, p. 50.

80. *Ibid.*

81. *Ibid.*

82. *Ibid.*

83. *Ibid.*, p. 155.

84. *Ibid.*, p. 130.

85. *Ibid.*, p. 131.

86. *Ibid.*, pp. 131–132.

87. *Ibid.*, p. 132.

88. *Ibid.*, p. 133.

89. *Ibid.*, p. 175.

90. M. de Montaigne, "Apology for Raymond Sebond," in *The Complete Works of Montaigne*, trans. Donald M. Frame (Stanford, 1958), p. 425.

91. Douglass, *op. cit.*, p. 139.
92. *Ibid.*, pp. 139–140.
93. *Ibid.*, p. 142.
94. *Ibid.*, p. 143.
95. *Ibid.*
96. *Ibid.*
97. Henson, *op. cit.*, pp. 3–7, 36–37.
98. Douglass, *op. cit.*, p. 143.
99. John L. Thomas, *The Liberator: William Lloyd Garrison* (Boston, 1963), p. 194.
100. Douglass, *op. cit.*, p. 275.
101. As quoted in the "Prologue," Thomas, *op. cit.*, p. 3.
102. Walter M. Merrill, *Against Wind and Tide: A Biography of Wm. Lloyd Garrison* (Cambridge, Mass., 1963), p. 39.
103. See Elkins, *op. cit.*, pp. xiii–xv.
104. *Supra.*, p. 42.
105. Douglass, *op. cit.*, pp. 147–148.
106. *Ibid.*, p. 155.
107. *Ibid.*, p. 155.
108. *Ibid.*, p. 187.

POSTSCRIPT TO CRUELTY

1. Reska Weiss, *Journey Through Hell* (London: Vallentine, Mitchell, 1961), p. 211.
2. Joachim Remak, ed. *The Nazi Years* (Englewood Cliffs, N.J.: Prentice-Hall, 1969), p. 159.
3. Frederick Douglass, *Life and Times* (New York: Collier Books, 1962), p. 186.
4. *Ibid.*, p. 155.

SELECTED BIBLIOGRAPHY

THE FOLLOWING LISTS ONLY THOSE BOOKS REFERRED TO IN FOOTNOTES.

Arendt, Hannah. *Eichmann in Jerusalem: A Report on the Banality of Evil.* New York: Viking Press, 1963.

Bettelheim, Bruno. *The Informed Heart: Autonomy in a Mass Age.* New York: The Free Press, 1961.

Birkhead, Edith. *The Tale of Terror.* New York: E.P. Dutton & Co., Inc., 1920.

Carmichael, Stokely, and Hamilton, Charles V. *Black Power: The Politics of Liberation in America.* New York: Vintage Books, 1967.

Cash, Wilbur J. *The Mind of the South.* New York: A.A. Knopf, 1941.

Cassell's New Latin Dictionary, ed. D. P. Simpson. New York: Funk & Wagnalls, 1959.

Céline, Louis-Ferdinand. *Journey to the End of the Night.* John H.P. Marks (trans.). London: Penguin Books, 1966.

Concise Oxford Dictionary of Current English, The. Adapted and revised from *The Oxford Dictionary* by H.W. Fowler, H.G. Le Mesurier, and E. McIntosh. London: Oxford University Press, 1949.

Conrad, Joseph. *A Conrad Argosy.* William McFee (introduction by). Garden City: Doubleday, Doran, & Co., 1942.

Douglass, Frederick. *Life and Times of Frederick Douglass: Written by Himself.* New York: Collier Books, 1962.

Du Bois, W.E. Burghardt. *The Souls of Black Folk: Essays and Sketches.* Greenwich, Connecticut: Fawcett Publications, 1967.

Eckermann, Johann Peter. *Conversations with Goethe.* John Oxenford (trans.) J.K. Moorhead (ed.). London: J.M. Dent & Sons, 1946.

Elkins, Stanley M. *Slavery: A Problem in American Institutional and Intellectual Life.* New York: Grosset and Dunlap, 1963.

Ellison, Ralph. *Invisible Man.* New York: Signet, 1965.

Fanon, Frantz. *The Wretched of the Earth.* Constance Farrington (trans.). New York: Evergreen Black Cat, 1968.

Ferris, William H. *The African Abroad.* New Haven, Connecticut: Yale University Press, 1913.

Fielding, Henry. *Joseph Andrews*. Martin C. Battestin (ed.). Middletown, Connecticut: Wesleyan University Press, 1967.

Freud, Anna. *The Ego and the Mechanisms of Defense*. London: New York International Publishers, 1946.

George, M. Dorothy. *London Life in the Eighteenth Century*. Middlesex, England: Penguin Books, 1966.

Harlan, Louis R. *Separate and Unequal: Public School Campaigns and Racism in the Southern Seaboard States 1901–1915*. New York: Atheneum, 1968.

Henson, Josiah. *Father Henson's Story of His Own Life*. New York: Corinth Books, 1962.

Heyerdahl, Thor. *Kon-Tiki: Across the Pacific by Raft*. F.H. Lyon (trans.). New York: Pocket Books, 1963.

Hogarth, William. *Analysis of Beauty*. Joseph Burke (ed.). Oxford: Clarendon Press, 1955.

Hogarth, William. MS 49, to be found in the British Museum.

In Their Own Words: A History of the American Negro 1619–1865. Vol. I of a projected three-volume set. Milton Meltzer (ed.) New York: Thomas Y. Crowell, 1967.

James, Henry. *Ghostly Tales of Henry James*. Leon Edel (ed.). New York: Grosset and Dunlap, 1963.

Kermode, Frank. *The Sense of an Ending: Studies in the Theory of Fiction*. New York: Oxford University Press, 1967.

Kierkegaard, S.K. *A Kierkegaard Anthology*. Robert Bretall (ed.). New York: Modern Library, 1946.

Lewis, Matthew G. *The Monk*. New York: Grove Press, 1959.

Lichtenberg, Georg Christoph. *Lichtenberg's Commentaries on Hogarth's Engravings*. Innes and Gustav Herdan (trans.). London: The Cresset Press, 1966.

Logan, Rayford W. *The Negro in the United States: A Brief History*. Princeton, New Jersey: D. Van Nostrand, 1957.

Maturin, Charles Robert. *Melmoth the Wanderer*. Lincoln, Nebraska: University of Nebraska Press, 1966.

Merrill, Walter M. *Against Wind and Tide: A Biography of Wm. Lloyd Garrison*. Cambridge, Massachusetts: Harvard University Press, 1963.

Montaigne, Michel de. *The Complete Works of Montaigne*. Donald M. Frame (trans.). Stanford, California: Stanford University Press, 1958.

Myrdal, Gunnar. *An American Dilemma: The Negro Problem and Modern Democracy*. New York: Harper & Brothers, 1944.

Nietzsche, Friedrich. *The Birth of Tragedy and the Genealogy of Morals*. Francis Golffing (trans.) Garden City: Doubleday & Company, 1956.

Otto, Rudolph. *The Idea of the Holy: An Inquiry into the Non-rational Factor in the Idea of the Divine and Its Relation to the Rational.* John W. Harvey (trans.). London: Oxford University Press, 1952.

Oxford English Dictionary, The. Vol. II ("C"). London: Oxford University Press, 1961.

Paris of Henry of Navarre, The. Nancy Roelker (ed.) Cambridge, Massachusetts: Harvard University Press, 1968.

Poe, Edgar Allan. *The Works of Edgar Allan Poe.* The quotations are taken from Volume Six ("Tales—Marvelous Adventure") in this ten-volume commemorative edition. New York: Funk & Wagnalls, 1904.

Praz, Mario. *The Romantic Agony.* Angus Davidson (trans.). Cleveland: Meridian, 1967.

Radcliffe, Ann. *The Mysteries of Udolpho*, abridged (with *The Castle of Otranto* by Horace Walpole and *Northanger Abbey* by Jane Austen). Andrew Wright, ed. New York: Holt, Rinehart and Winston, 1963.

Sade, D.A.F. de. *Les Crimes de l'amour*, Volume III in the collection *D.A.F. de Sade: Oeuvres complètes.* Paris: J.J. Pauvert, 1966.

——————. *Dialogue entre un pretre et un moribond et autres opuscules; Oxtiern; Ecrits politiques*, Volume VIII in the collection *D.A.F. de Sade: Oeuvres complètes.* Paris: J.J. Pauvert, 1966.

——————. *Juliette, or, Vice Amply Rewarded.* A revised and edited abridgement of Pieralessandro Casavini's translation. London: Gold Star Publications, 1966.

——————. *The Marquis de Sade.* Compiled and translated by Richard Seaver and Austryn Wainhouse. New York: Grove Press, 1966.

——————. *The Marquis de Sade: Selected Letters.* W. J. Strachan (trans.); Margaret Crosland (ed.). London: Peter Owen, 1965.

——————. *The 120 Days of Sodom.* Translator's name not revealed. North Hollywood, California: Brandon House, 1967.

Sarbin, Theodore R. "The Culture of Poverty, Social Identity, and Cognitive Outcomes," an article to appear in *Psychological Factors in Poverty*, V.L. Allen (ed.). Chicago, Illinois: Markham, 1969.

Seton, Ernest Thompson. *Wild Animals I Have Known.* New York: Bantam, 1946.

Stoker, Bram. *Dracula.* New York: Modern Library, n.d.

Stoic and Epicurean Philosophers, The: The Complete Writings of Epicurus, Epictetus, Lucretius, Marcus Aurelius. Whitney J. Oates (ed.). New York: Random House, 1940.

Stowe, Harriet Beecher. *Uncle Tom's Cabin, or, Life Among the Lowly.* New York: Harper and Row, 1965.

Tannenbaum, Frank. *Slave and Citizen: The Negro in America.* New York: A.A.Knopf, 1947.

Thomas, John L. *The Liberator: William Lloyd Garrison; A Biography.* Boston: Little, Brown & Co., 1963.

Vampire, an Anthology, The. Ornella Volta and Valeria Riva (eds.). London: Pan Books, 1965.

Vrba, Rudolf, and Bestic, Alan. *I Cannot Forgive.* London: The Byron Press, 1964.

Waskow, Arthur I. *From Race Riot to Sit-In, 1919 and the 1960s: A Study in the Connections between Conflict and Violence.* Garden City: Anchor, 1967.

Woodward, C. Vann. *The Strange Career of Jim Crow.* New York: Oxford University Press, 1957.

INDEX OF NAMES

Names appearing below in quotation marks are characters in fiction.

SUBJECT INDEX